ADDICTED TO TH

What were you thinking? A question I've been
over again. Sometimes by my parents, sometimes by f
claimed to be like everybody else, I'm not. But I do re
else. Just normal, average, just fade into the backgrour
viewed as the same. I felt I was different, not in a bad way or an odd ball, but just different. I didn't feel I felt the same way other people did. Think the same.

From years of questioning things I couldn't explain to other people. Thinking I must be mad, driving myself mad in the process. It took nearly two decades, five different counsellors, an alter ego, an SIA license and nine overdoses to finally come to a point where I understood.

I'm not like everybody else, but there are other people like me... Seb James

His story is unlike the others because he is unlike the majority, loved by some, hated by some, but known by all. He is the man with more lives than a cat, more luck than the Irish and a heart that just keeps going no matter what. His story is entertaining and in places tragic. His alter ego is a fucking law unto himself. You worry about him and at the same time you think he's capable of looking after himself. You don't what or who is going to turn up at any point, will you get Seb the thoughtful, intelligent, quick witted and relatively charming fella who's there for a laugh or will you get Wimbo? The ounce a night sniffing lunatic who can't be trusted.

ADDICTED TO THE LIFE

Welcome To My World

Well firstly, thank you for purchasing my book, unless we've actually managed to generate enough notoriety to have a version in Waterstones and you're just reading it whilst waiting for your other half to finish wondering around the shops, in which case go up to the counter and pay for the book you cheeky fucker.

When you set out on something you don't really know where it's going to end up, there's no set plan or designed outcome and you have to just get up, get on with it and hope for the best. You don't get a road map for life or a list of cheats and hacks like you do with GTA; life and everything in it is just a massive case of trial and error.

To let you know a little bit about what you're in for with my book I best give you a bit of brief information to help get yourself prepared. This is a book about the world of door work, but we are going to go behind the doors and look into all the things that you as a member of the public would never get to see or experience for yourself. If you think that the world of nightclubs and late night entertainment is just a bit of fun, and it would be a lot more enjoyable for everyone if we just had nicer bouncers, then you are a fucking moron. You need to read this book, have a tiny peak into exactly what we have to go through, and the shit we've had to do to cover for the people that expect us to get stabbed or jumped for the princely sum of £10phr (if you're lucky.)

You're going to be seeing everything through my eyes including the way I interpreted the situations and the people I have had to deal with. This book spans the better part of the decade I have spent involved in the nightclub and bar industry. The fact you're essentially coming along for the ride whilst I drive it seems only fair that you get a completely honest, and uncensored look at me as a person, so I'll give you a full run down of who I am and what has lead me to this point. I'll do my best not to bore you too much with that bit as I'm sure you're eager to get to the bit in the book that talks about drugs, steroids, court cases, stabbings and women. This book is like me: it comes with no filter.

This book is in no way intended to be a swipe at the bouncers of today or portray them in a negative light (even though the entire protocol and requirements for what consisted of a 'decent' bouncer went out the fucking window the second the Olympics came to London and every fucker and their mate was suddenly given a license and a job!) the intention is to shine a light on the state of the industry, how it's changed and the bull shit we have to deal with from managers, club owners, and companies whose only real concern is their money and will just as easily replace you before they will even consider helping you out. This is not to say that I haven't gained a lot from my time on the doors, I have some of the closest friends in the world all due to the bond that gets created between doormen. I have business partners and opportunities I would have never gotten if it wasn't for my time in this profession. So don't fret it's not all doom and gloom.

ADDICTED TO THE LIFE

About me.... I made the decision a long time ago when I first started writing a book, that I would hold absolutely nothing back. Any of my friends and the people I have worked with through the last decade knows that I say whatever I feel, and I have no second thoughts about openly discussing my less than pleasant activities or habits. I changed the concept and style several times, trying to find what would work best. People around me think this concept came about over a few months, but truth is it's been something in the pipe line for at least two years. The only way this was going to work was if it was a truly honest, real story and it was going to have to involve me talking about my life outside of the clubbing world. I never intended to write some autobiography and attempt to thrust myself into the never ending cycle of z-list wannabe celebrities, but without a bit of me then it was just a series of stories moving from one club to the next. To be honest when I first read that version of this book, well fuck me it was dull, it just lacked that something that makes you want to keep turning the pages.

So in for a penny out for a pound as they say........

I remember pink. Pink everywhere and on everything. I remember looking up and there's this doily thing, one of those toilet roll covers your grandparents like to use to 'hide' the fact they used toilet paper from people. I remember just looking up and it was staring at me, this little pale face, its eyes just fucking locked on me. Not in a menacing way or a sympathetic way, just these dead painted eyes staring right back at me.

I was in bits sobbing on the floor, uncontrollably, widely sobbing. I couldn't talk, I couldn't stand up, I was just broken. There was nothing anyone could say or do that was going to help. I didn't know you could do that to another human being, and I didn't know someone, something could hurt that much, deeply, mentally, emotionally, just a never ending feeling of pain and despair. I didn't say anything, I couldn't, and if I could who would understand? Who would listen and be able to tell me it was alright, that I would get over it or at least learn to cope with it. I'm a kid, what the fuck do I know?

I was first given pain killers when I was about ten or eleven years old and the timing of this could not have been worse. I had a very small and select circle of friends, and for reasons that are still unknown and incomprehensible to me as a ten or eleven year old, they simply woke up one day and decided they didn't want to be my friends anymore. I don't remember the exact circumstances around this time, but I had just spent a season playing baseball for a local team and had been selected to an all stars training camp. It was one of those camps that you have scouts and other agents looking at the possible next generation of major and minor league baseball players. It was on this day that I proceeded to have the worst day of my fucking life, and dislocated my knee due to a fast ball that I was unable to get out of the way of. Why did I not get out the way of it? I was busy thinking about how shit my day was going, the next thing I know I was crumpled on the floor clutching my knee and thinking okay maybe earlier wasn't so bad.

I remember him looking into my eyes. I remember looking over at him and thinking 'what is he looking at?' I'm crumpled on the floor this mess of a human looking like a pile of

ADDICTED TO THE LIFE

dirty clothes just dumped in the corner waiting to be washed. My insides felt like they had been mangled, I was a state, a broken machine with bits strewn everywhere. And there he is just looking at me. I remember because I actually saw compassion in his eyes, they were full of emotion. I hadn't seen that in my own eyes, let alone anyone else's since God knows when. He ran over and sat next to me nuzzled in and laid down, he looked after me; he cared at a time where I didn't care about myself. But what do I know right? I'm a kid.

I'm popping painkillers for my knee like tic tacs for God knows how long, and then I get all the shit from my 'friends' at school: I'm not quite the same person I am now as I was back then. As hard as it is for most of my friends, and the people who know me now to believe back then I didn't swear, I was a calm, shy and caring little boy, I was also very insecure and incredibly vulnerable when it came to what people thought of me. I'm not going to into a hundred percent detail of all the things that happened then, mainly because I don't remember certain things. One of the things I learnt later in life with my councillor (yeah I'll get into that more later on) was that some parts we instinctively block out, it's a defence mechanism.

So I'm about fifteen I think, and I've been using painkillers and weed to help deal with the ever increasing anxiety I have about day to day life. Somewhere around this point in time my mum and dad separated. Before I go any further I'm going to say a few things in this next bit that may sound as though I didn't like my parents or that I hold some ill will towards them, I do not. People always try to establish what your parents are like and use that as a basis to understand you. I don't get that. I think that's bullshit to an extent. Your parents are parents, and it's a job they get given with absolutely no training or prior work experience, and to cap off the pressure they have the ability to directly affect your entire life. The best thing I ever heard when someone tried to describe parenting was that they try to make you remember the good and not just the bad. There is only going to be bad, they're human you're human.

My parents were my parents and our relationship is ours and ours alone. My dad worked his ass off every fucking day and we had food, new clothes, holidays (4 times to Disneyworld before we were 15) to different countries, he refereed our football games, dropped me to baseball every Saturday and to this day he still comes along to see me do stand up gigs. My mum was the same; she supported everything we wanted to be involved in. So you can't just look at the time it didn't go right, that's not fair.

My parents' separation was not swift nor was it pleasant; it was a long drawn out and unpleasant affair that had us all living together for quite some time whilst things got sorted out. One of the main things that shaped my mind set about life and how I was going to deal with things which arose out of that situation. My mum and dad were both hurting from that situation, but unfortunately they didn't deal with it in the best possible way.

Having a conversation with my brother he said how my mum had asked him to live with her after the separation. I had had no conversation along these lines with my mother, and figured she did not want me to live with her, so later I spoke with my dad and asked to live

ADDICTED TO THE LIFE

with him. At that time I was a kid and I was hurting and I didn't understand. I learnt later my mum had assumed that I would live with her and that was why she didn't sit down and talk with me. In her mind she already had her youngest with her. Having spoken with my dad he was thrilled that I wanted to live him. I think being that my mum had filed for divorce, I believed he was afraid he was going to literally lose everything that he had.

Unfortunately my parents were not at the point of being pleasant to each other. During an argument my dad told my mum that I had asked to live with him, and my mum said that was untrue. So what was the only sensible thing to do? Call down your son and make him stand in front of you both and tell your mum that you didn't want to live with her. Yeah that was fucking pleasant! My mum was devastated. She would come into my room in the mornings before I would be getting up for college and stand at the end of my bed and ask me why I hated her. I can't remember how long that lasted, but that was how I started my days for a period of time. It still plays on my mind today - I will point out that myself and my mum have a fantastic relationship today and she is my biggest supporter and is always trying to find some way to help me with whatever I'm doing, she really is my number one fan and I love her very much – I would stay in bed until the house was empty, skip college and spend my days hanging around the local park, woodlands or recreation centre. My day consisted of trying to figure out a way to get money and look after myself. Obviously this involved stealing things and weed, both buying and selling and smoking copious amounts of it.

I found my pain relief and it worked for me. It gave me the ability to just cope – it made you feel invincible, but that wasn't what was really going on- in all honesty I didn't think about it, because I didn't care. If not feeling fuck all was how my life carried on working, then so be it.

It would turn out to be a near fourteen year dependency with drugs. The reason I'm telling you this? Looking at my time as a doorman, it is only the last three years that I was not running on drugs daily. I managed to work out that it was a five year period where I had some type of drug in my system every single day!

I've walked into and away from some of the most toxic situations and people imaginable. People I considered family who, when it came down to it were just out for themselves, users, ego maniacs who were never going to achieve anything, but needed to feel superior in their small, fake, little worlds. Years of brotherhood gone without a second thought.

I remember watching a couple of different things that really connected with me. The first was an ESPN special called The Wrestler about a former professional wrestler and addict named Scott Hall. I told my mum if she ever wanted to try to understand me, and then watch that – I don't think she ever did. The second was on an episode of Dog the Bounty Hunter when he talked about one of his sons. I think it was a little boy called Zebediah who was born premature, and Dog stood watching him at the hospital in a ventilator and a nurse comes in to give him an injection. The nurse pulls out this big syringe and gives the baby an injection. Dog asks why he's smiling and the nurse says that when all he's known is pain,

ADDICTED TO THE LIFE

how is he supposed to know anything else? That moment alone triggered so many memories in that one tiny fragment of my life, that for the first time in years I broke down sobbing on my lounge floor.

So this is me: socially maladjusted, masking my feelings of helplessness by bluffing my way through life and stifling the inner screams of my insecurities with drugs and now I'm getting an SIA license to work as a bouncer. Why? It was always the biggest guys I had remembered watching on TV. Professional wrestlers, athletes, strongmen, they modelled what I grew up idolising, they were big therefore fearless. They were too big, too violent, and too tough to have fears and insecurities. This would fix all my problems, but what did I know? I was functioning addict masquerading as an adult.

Firstly let me introduce myself, my name is Wimbo Slice and later in the book you'll find out how I came to be. I am the other half of Seb's mild split personality – the one lasting reminder of years of drug abuse. If you thought doing DMT opened up some new dimensions and allowed your psyche to explore the vast parameters of the experimental realm you thought only existed in sci fi films. Well have you ever wondered what would happen if the altered you followed you back into your subsequent home reality? HELLO MOTHERFUKERS I'VE COME FOR A VISIT... My job is to tell you what Seb was really thinking and didn't actually want to put in the book as it might be a bit controversial. So look out for my little comments throughout the book...

ADDICTED TO THE LIFE

Time To Go To School

I was just starting my second year at college – I had decided to return to education after a substantial absence in a bid to at least try and do something more with my life (work wise) – and had spent the last 2 years working as bar man/chef at a pub and had figured I spent enough time having to deal with loud mouth drunks, so why not get paid more money for it.

Ladies and gentlemen I can honestly say that my FOUR day course to become an SIA qualified and government standard approved door supervisor was the most pointless four days of my fucking life! The course teaches you absolutely nothing that you can actually use in a dangerous situation or in any real time situation! Well, it may be a bit harsh to say it was completely useless as it did get me my first job offer from the course instructor Chris. Chris was a very knowledgeable guy, he's ex services and was at the time one of the directors of a very busy security company – I'll get more into my time there in the next chapter.

You were walked through all the basic elements you would be expected to know to be a bouncer, how to stand, how to try and keep yourself as shielded from a possible surprise attack, the basic things expected from your employer and your colleagues and then all the stuff the SIA make you learn that is not practical, but will provide them with complete legal cover should you injure someone or be injured yourself – crafty fuckers!

I'll give you an example: the average nightclub will have about six/seven doormen working in it dependant on the size of the venue. Under SIA approved operating procedures it requires a MINIMUM of SEVEN, that's right SEVEN bouncers to remove ONE person from the venue. If you see a fight break out in the club, the SIA operating procedure states that you should radio for assistance, calmly go up to the fight and wait for assistance to arrive. ONLY when there is the approved amount of security personnel, should you then attempt to resolve the situation. You are told to resolve the situation using verbal communication and if that fails only once you have exhausted all other avenues are you to calmingly take the offender by the wrist in a stern yet gentle manner and walk him away from the situation. Yeah this is the guy whose drunk fuck knows how many Stella, jager bombs, tequilas and 3 grams of bugle who is currently kicking the fuck out of another human being, so he is going to be more compliant with you and if he's not, well that's your fault as you clearly didn't follow the GOVERNMENT APPROVED PROCEDURES.

The SIA governing body who layout the government procedures for how we should do our job are not made up of a collection of current or former security personnel, but of normal people, none of whom have ever actually worked in a nightclub or bar in a security role in their entire lives. That to me is the equivalent of going into hospital for surgery and the janitor pops up to do your consult, he's never done an operation before, nor does he have any medical knowledge or experience, but he is sure that he knows the best way, so okay, you crack on son- it's absolutely fucking ridiculous!

ADDICTED TO THE LIFE

If you work as a bouncer, a fight kicks off and you just walk up and stand there waiting for your other members of staff to turn up whilst the club or bar you're in gets trashed due to this fight, I guarantee your ass will not have a job come the end of that shift. The managers and/or owners will fire you on the fucking spot, because in their eyes you are not doing your job, but you've following the guidelines and procedures set out in your training, so you'll be okay right? No, you're fired and whilst you're trying to find a new venue to work at, the management who've just fired you (for doing what your told to do in your training) will let every other club know that you're a liability and all the other bouncers in town will be told you're shy when it comes to stepping into a violent situation. Bottom line is: you are fucked!

The four day course is spread over two weeks, two days per week. It cost me at the time £260 to sit my exams and do the course. You are then charged another £240 to apply for your license. So yeah you've passed the exam, but if you actually want to use those qualifications for work, then you're charged again. Once you have your qualification and to make a bit of extra cash out of you, every three years you have to pay another £250 to renew your license or you can't continue working. How many other jobs out there charge you to keep working? It's an absolute joke! (By the way, the price for your door supervisors' course is now a little over £600.)

Oh and if you have ever wondered why you look at some bouncers and see someone who looks like they couldn't knock out a decent wank let alone back you up in a violent situation, it's because the main selling point of the course is and I quote 'If you can speak English and tie your own shoes, you're pretty much guaranteed to pass.' When I did my exam I was told the only person who had ever failed was a Chinese guy who spoke no English whatsoever.

Long story short, course done, exam passed, ridiculous fees paid, license granted....now for the fun part.

I had been a gym enthusiast for about four years and had got my weight up to a solid/ripped 13st – not that big in the world of door work – so there was only one thing for it. STEROIDS. If I was going to have to remove people from a nightclub in the midst of some massive brawl, or would have to scoop some drunken Shamu like whale off the girls' bathroom floor, then it would be beneficial for me to be considerably bigger than the average person.

The course was fucking bullshit..... The steroids were brilliant!

ADDICTED TO THE LIFE

New Boy

As I stated earlier my first job fresh out of training was for the company Chris was a director of. I started off being darted about from place to place for the first three months. I had brief stint at Walkabout – a very cheap Australian themed club – before the manager wished for me to be moved to somewhere else. Apparently he wanted either big, massive, hulking, behemoths or pretty boys – good news, I'm small and ugly – so off I went.

When you first start you really are left to do the simplest of things and in true new boy fashion you get those things wrong. Not from being inept or stupid, but you just second guess everything and end up over complicating the littlest issues. It does take a bit of time to find your groove and get into a rhythm. Oh, and for any of you guys who got your licenses recently and are sat there thinking 'I've been fine, I'm already doing it like a pro' you're fucking not, you're probably the team wanker who everyone thinks is an arrogant little cunt.

Working at V club (it's since been bought and renamed and rebranded as something else) was and still is the most fun I've ever had at any job. The club was rammed from start to finish each and every night it was open. Monday was student night, Tuesday was international night, Friday was just Friday night and Saturday I think was called Aura Saturdays– It was exactly the same as Friday night, but with the addition of different lighting. I know, I know, marketing geniuses.

The bouncers there were regarded by all the other bouncers in town as a different breed, they were literally the last throw backs to the ever dying system of slap first ask questions later era of door work. Now before you get all judgemental and start tutting about over excessive bouncers, V was one of the busiest, if not the busiest club in town, it regularly held over 1200 people in it, and when you have that many people in one place you have fights. The average amount of fights we had to deal with per night was between 11 and 14 and that's not girly handbags and hissy fits, that is full blown fighting, punches, kicks, belts being taken off and whipped at your head, glasses and bottles being thrown at you. For us optimum fight time was between 00:30 – 02:00. That's point when people are now pissed enough to really not care or think about what they're doing. They are well and truly drunk, rowdy and have little to no inhibitions left.

The team at V was an interesting mix of characters. Rudi was on the front door (he was in charge.) Rudi was an older guy when you think about the average age of door staff; he had a significantly well paying job and just seemed to work on the doors because he enjoyed having a laugh with the boys. Danny was the internal (his job was to move you on rotation and cover you for a fag break.) Danny was also the most offensive and racist guy I think I've ever met, he had no filter and absolutely no people skills. When I got my first shift at V and turned up early for my induction and walk around, the first thing Danny said to me upon hearing my name was "not another fucking foreigner?!" I had a different name then. The rest of the team included: Scott now the other half of my bromance (we'll get more into that later on in the book) Taz, who became one of my closest mates and I'm still good friends with

ADDICTED TO THE LIFE

today, Polish Rob, Cat the crazy Romanian, Bart another crazy polish guy and Lee who was just Lee – who was also the most ripped guy I think I've ever seen, the guy was in incredible shape and would put pretty much all of the little pretty boy wannabes who post top less picks on instagram to shame - and he was by far the most pleasant member of the team. The rest of the team would be made up of a host of fill in guys for when the team went up to fifteen doormen on the big nights.

I fucking loved turning up to work there, it was a night in and night out fun for a guy like me. I'd been brought up with the notion that there was never a need for violence. If someone was threatening or being abusive, then the best thing to change the situation was to change your location, just walk away and don't let someone see that they got to you. What did I discover the first time a fight kicked off? I fucking loved hitting someone. I instantly fell in love with the feeling of power that would rush into you. It did not matter how shit a day you had or what the fuck was going on in your personal life, when you physically outmatch another person there is no better short term feeling in the world – it was like getting an instant fix. Over the course of waiting for certificates to come through from finishing my SIA to starting work as a bouncer, I had upgraded my steroids. I had started with a simple oral called Dianabol, but had since moved on to injections. I believe Test 100 was my drug of choice of that moment in time.

Now to say V was a bit different and real eye opener would be an understatement. The club was owned by Richard Carr, a man who has been bankrupt, black listed and investigated by the police for everything from fraud to money laundering to drug smuggling – I'll point out none of it ever stuck and he continues to operate as a successful businessman today. The majority opinion of most people is that he is a fucking asshole. I'll be honest, I didn't ever speak to him whilst I worked there, but we did have an interesting exchange and meeting when I left V but I'll save that until a bit later. The club was managed by Steve, the deputy manager Karl and later on my school friend Daryl started working there as another manager. All of this was overseen by Jim, Richard his right hand man and equally as shady business confidant. Steve was Steve; he ran the club, kept out of the way and let us get on with things. Daryl was one for the door team, he always backed you up and ignored the fact most of us were off our nuts when working. Karl was, how do I put this nicely; he was a two faced, bitter, little fag. And that's the nicest thing I could actually say about him.

As I said the team was full of characters and everyone had a little something off about them. There was also a clear divide between the door staff and the bar staff. If you did something that the bar staff thought was a bit heavy handed or unjust, they would sing to the management without a second thought.

I'm not saying bar staff should lie or cover up for door staff, but we all work in the same place and we're all trying to get through the night with as little drama as possible, but it's us that get the physical abuse from customers, it's us they have the vendetta against, it's us that has to drag them kicking and screaming from the venue when they are rude or abusive to the bar staff, it's us that they wait for in the car park at 3am with their group of mates. So when you see us do something out of the corner of your eye and you're not quite sure why or

ADDICTED TO THE LIFE

what you saw, then keep your fucking mouth shut, because the next time you're in serious trouble of being hurt, we will remember that you ran your mouth off and will we walk as slowly as humanly possible to get to you.

Your weekends were set out as standard, Fridays and Saturdays were your typical club nights, no different set up from anywhere else really. We just had a bigger venue and an owner with deeper pockets to draw in 'celebrity' acts. Mondays were student night. This meant your night was filled with eighteen year olds who had just started drinking, had just moved away from home and seemed to think they were now some sort of badass. Now to give you a brief idea of what awaited you should you act like a cunt, give it the big man and start challenging the door staff to a fight. At 6ft1 and 13.5st I was height to weight ratio wise one of the smaller guys on the team when I started, most of the guys there were 6ft+ and weighed over the 16st mark. The only height restricted guy on the team was Taz, but what he lacked in height he made up for in power and being an utter fucking psycho when shit kicked off – loved that crazy fucker to pieces then and still do now.

The guys at the club who were deemed full time (worked all four nights) were Scott, Danny and I. Everybody else would do two or three nights. As I said about Danny earlier he was an interesting guy, but I got on well with him and still do, but he was an out and out bully. International nights were by far the worst, he would just pick on the little Arabic guys that would come in, he'd openly insult them knowing they couldn't understand him, when bored he would make them do push ups outside in the street before they could come in. When shit kicked off Danny would be there in the mix with you, so despite whether or not you agreed with or liked about him and how he kept himself amused during a shift, you knew he would jump in when needed. He was a bastard for taking an extra swipe at someone you were trying to control or remove. Numerous times someone would turn around and spit at me, thinking it was me who slapped them after Danny had slapped them in the back of the head or taken a sly dig at them and then walked away.

Other than what was deemed by other clubs to be an overly aggressive door team, V was known for drugs and violence – I don't mean just the customers when talking drugs. I'll be the first to admit I was one of a host of guys who was taking steroids (the old doorman cliché.) I was however the doorman that put everyone else to shame when it came to drugs. Not just an intense steroid cycle that saw me gain about 3 stone in a few months, but my recreational and 'work' drug taking was on another planet. I took absolutely anything and more of it than anybody else. In addition to my steroid cycle, at work my usual cocktail was three or four epidrine, two T5's, some clenbuterol and usually a bump of coke if there was any going, all washed down with an unlimited supply of red bull.

The funniest thing and the thing I remember most about V was that a lot of the guys had a problem with needles. You had this group of huge, tattooed guys and yet some of them would be terrified to do a quick injection. So a couple of us would turn up to work about fifteen minutes early to help each other with our steroid injections. We would try and go into the toilets and do it in there, so occasionally one of the guys would walk in and see a parade

ADDICTED TO THE LIFE

of bare asses bent over the sinks and one serious looking doorman behind them in a compromising position saying "stop squirming, I'm not going in very deep, just take it."

So when you're wondering why when you look around the club and you can see doormen physically shaking, with eyes dilated and practically frothing at the mouth waiting for a fight that may be why. So be careful for fuck sake.

One of the problems I developed was experimentation, (calm down I'll get to those stories later) I'm talking about drugs, specifically what we considered your door work drugs, epidrine and T5. I used to take 3 epidrine at the start of my shift and that would normally see me through. If I was going to grab an extra few hours at a late late venue then I'd pop T5 as well.

So I'm stood at the top of the stairs leading up and overlooking the main dance floor and one of the boys, I don't remember who exactly, says they have a mate who said if you take 4 epidrine, your body will literally explode. Well fuck it I had to prove him wrong so I popped 4 there and then. After about 30mins nothing had happened, not a single thing, didn't feel any different to when I started, no more alert than usual. So the smart thing to do was to see what would actually happen if I took more – I know, I know it really wasn't that smart. I took my 5th pill and waited to see what or when something might happen.

Well, fuck me did something happen! I didn't feel anything in my chest, not a hint of an explosion brewing. However, things south of the border began to get interesting. I'm not talking about around the back, no no I'm talking around the front. My fucking balls literally began to shrink and try to retract back inside me! I was stood at the top of the stairs with one hand down my trousers cupping my balls and pulling them ever so gently forward to stop them retracting. I did not know how this situation could possibly get any worse. Oh good a fight gets called over the radio and it just so happens to be in the smoking area – the furthest possible point from where I am stood. So off I go, hand still firmly clenched ever so gently round tender bollocks whilst running at full speed through a packed nightclub. I get to the incident just in time to tackle one guy (yes one armed as I am still cradling the family jewels) and take him to the floor, knee onto chest, arm twisted behind him and perched firmly on top of drunken moron, who takes one look up at me and as I'm screaming "don't fucking try anything" he looks at my other hand still down my pants and says "what the fuck man, dude whatever, I don't want that kind of trouble, just keep that thing away from me."

There was one time at the start of a shift Karl called me over and asked me if I thought Dan was alright because he didn't seem to be able to stop moving when standing on the spot. He was shaking and twitching like a junkie waiting for a fix. I looked at him and said he was fine. I asked Karl for a red bull and when I stuck my hand out it was shaking so much you would have thought I had Parkinson's disease. He just stared at my hand in disbelief and walked away.

I pretty much ran on a cocktail of illegal, legal and soon to be illegal drugs. I was necking valiums and muscle relaxants to sleep, getting through my day to day life with

ADDICTED TO THE LIFE

steroids and clenbuterol, my work nights were epidrine and T5's and if it was a night off, then all aboard the cocaine express! Choo choo.

It wasn't always on the nights he was off that he was on the train Choo Choo.

I have friends who when on a night out like to have a cheeky bag or two, that's cute to get you going. On a night off I would go through between eight and fourteen grams (fourteen grams is a half ounce of coke) on my own and I only stopped when the supply ran dry. I was a walking biohazard and everyone knew it. I'm not saying that door work was the reason for my own drug abuse as I was already a drug dependant mess before arriving at that junction in my life. Door work just gave me something to occupy my time whilst on drugs.

In amongst all the fighting and drama with members of management and bar staff, you had two things that filled up the majority of your shift. The regular faces who came through the door every night and the ladies – we'll get to the ladies in a little bit.

When I started Taz made sure to introduce me to the people who were worth knowing and were allowed 'special' treatment. The main group that spent every night with us was a coalition of guys from Kurdistan, Turkey, Albania and Iraq. The most noticeable character was a guy called Kaz. Kaz was the guy who seemed to be calling all the shots on a night out. He appeared no bigger than about 5ft5, looked like he weighed less than 8st, but the guy was surrounded by people hanging off his every word, he had women clambering all over him and as I later experienced had absolutely no problem taking apart someone well over 6ft. In short, the guy was a tiny stick of dynamite that would take on all comers of all shapes and sizes, if they wanted to fight, then they definitely had a fight on their hands.

Kaz was also one of our favourite guys to have in the club. Why? He treated everyone who worked there with the upmost respect. It did not matter if you were the owner or the glass collector, he would say hello, offer to buy you a drink or a cigarette or anything he had. He was by far the nicest guy I had dealt with.

I've known Kaz for years now, he is not just some guy I met in a club that I occasionally say hello to. He's given me a job at one of his businesses; we've been to dinner, out for birthdays and other celebrations together. If I remember one thing about all the years I've known him that stands out, it's not the times he got a bit carried away, and we've helped him out by hiding him away or gently nudging him in the right direction, it is most definitely those fucking neon bright suits he used to wear. Fuck me; the man was like a light house beaconing the drunken wenches towards him.

Numerous times we would hide Kaz in a room or office space after he had been involved in an incident and then slide him out the back door before the police had arrived. Mysteriously enough, whenever the police arrived the CCTV footage seemed not to be working.

For those of you that aren't really that familiar with how the night club scene works let me try and illustrate that for you now. If you have ever wondered why the week before you watched a guy practically cave some poor fellas head in and then the next week he is up

ADDICTED TO THE LIFE

in the VIP drinking and partying with all his buddies, well it's simple, he's the club dealer. If you think that the clubs don't have someone peddling drugs for them in the club, then you are a naive idiot and you should stop reading this book. Cocaine and clubbing goes hand in fucking hand. The main problem is that after a while the in house dealers become comfortable and get less and less subtle about what they are doing and it becomes a little problematic. When a customer comes up to you and says that guy over there is openly dealing drugs, you can't turn around and say, oh don't worry he's our in house dealer. The ironic thing is, when you turn up to work you are told under no circumstances that you are allowed to be on drugs or do drugs or have drugs in your system, the club has a zero tolerance policy on drugs. However, the management are all in the office sniffing their fucking brains out, the owner is currently suspected of international drug smuggling, the in house dealers are in the club knocking out bags left, right and centre whilst putting aside the clubs cut, the owners/ managers friends are all coming in and using the key for the disabled toilets so they can do their coke in privacy, but you the doorman, if you're suspected of being anywhere near a drug, your ass is fired. Just a tad ironic to me. Keep the drugs out, unless they're our drugs or our friends. But to be fair I didn't really abide by that strict code of conduct.

The unfortunate lesson in life is that not everyone in your life is in it for the long haul. Sometimes you have to walk away from the toxic. No matter how much febreeze you lacquer on shit, it's still gonna fucking stink.

So Danny needs a favour, something to do with one of his windows, so I call my mate and we go round to take a look. We get some measurements, get a price and arrange to come back and sort it out the next day.

Dan and my mate – we'll call him Mr X – hit it off, they are essentially the same person, over macho, die hard Chelsea fans, who think unless your language involves swearing then that is an admittance of homosexuality.

Window fitted and we all decide to go for a beer. Now me and Mr X have been close friends for five years and therefore know things about each other that are more personal and not freely shared with everyone.

I decided it was best for me to take over this part of the book as Seb does have a tendency to get a little emotional at times and his personal feelings can bubble up to the surface. It's his main flaw. The poor fucker cares too much and invests too much in the wrong people.

I deleted the original passage that was in this books original draft. Let me make this point clear before people try and put their own bullshit spin or reasoning on it. It was done for one reason and one reason alone. The original although it clearly showed why the incident ended our friendship and highlighted and explained the fucking bullshit and gutless move made by friend X it also took down his then girlfriend under a degree of friendly fire and I will not expose, bring up or talk about someone's personal life when I have been asked

ADDICTED TO THE LIFE

not to. Years on and I am still a man of my word. It's a crying shame the same could not be said for other people.

I lost a friend who was like family, a family that was like my own and a mother figure who had literally become a second mum. That is what I miss the most. Jax you are a fighter, but first and for most you're a mother and it was a privilege to be your favourite son for a while.

It's been years since we spoke and I've had nothing to do with him, his family or any of our so called mutual friends since.

I learnt a lot from my friendship with Mr X. sadly it was pretty one sided in the friendship department. An example you ask? So one time X is working at a shop and it seems to be going ok. I get a call off him saying I need to come round after my door shift urgently as it's an emergency. I go round and he asks me to drive him to his work. I say sure and we jump in my car. I get to his work and park where he tells me to. He disappears inside and then appears later telling me to pop my trunk open. A bit of rummaging and he's back in the car. I get back to his and he starts to unload my car. His emergency? He had stashed some TV screens out the back door to take and decided it would be better to come back in my car in case we got seen on CCTV so they wouldn't track his license plate... Good friend yeah?

When I was starting out, one of the main focuses of entertainment when trying to get through a shift was the ladies. In the beginning doormen were still seen as something of a novelty, a valuable commodity for a young, attractive girl to have at her side. If you were a girl in a club anywhere in town and you were known to be seeing or involved with a doorman, then you were pretty much as safe as you could possibly be. It's a matter of respect between doormen, we watch out for each other and the people that we care about. If you were dumb enough to come up to a girl that one of my friends was involved with or I was involved with, then you my boy were in for a very bad time. I don't mean if you looked at, or came up chatted to her but when you didn't take the hint or thought it was acceptable to grab ass or call her a slut when she shot you down, you were not only in for a very unpleasant exit from where ever you so happened to be, but your face and behaviour would be passed onto which ever doorman that lady was connected to. Trust me when they spotted you in a club or bar things were going to be even worse for you.

The most notable type of girls and the regulars you had at the club were what we ever so delicately called the 'shake and fake' girls they're hilarious. These were girls who were only using you for the sheer convenience and skill set you could offer. They wanted VIP treatment, queue jumps, free entry, wristbands and any type of discount or freebie they could get their hands on. Why did we let them get away with this? Well it's simple; in return for those freebies you generally got sexual favours. A blow job in the toilets whilst on your break, a cheeky hand job through your trousers whilst you were stood on position – trust me this happens as I've been wanked off in just as many clubs as I have at home on a lonely night in with youporn – and of course coming home with you after your shift for sex. The funny thing is most of the girls who did this seemed to think they were in some way different

ADDICTED TO THE LIFE

from the other girls who did this, that they were special and that you should almost be grateful for them choosing you. Ladies, I'm sorry to tell you that most doormen had a couple of girls if not several that did this for them. You ladies were not the VIPs you seemed to think you were

I'll take a quick walk down memory lane with you. When I first started I had no real idea that girls operated in this way. That simply by standing by a stair way or dance floor in skin tight, neon top somehow gave you an aura of prestige (I was a little naive or clueless it could be said in this type of situation) I had spent some time battling depression and the before section of my personal life with women wasn't phenomenal before door work, but I'll get more into that later. The first time a girl asked me 'how she got in VIP' I just stood there and repeated the price of wrist bands about 6 times before she gave up and walked up to another more streetwise bouncer.

As we are on the subject, let me just jump into present day for a moment. If you have spent the last six or so years coming into nightclubs every weekend, gone home with various knob head members of the local pretty boy, look how much money my mummy and daddy gave me for the club, then why are you sat on face book complaining that there are no decent men in town? There are decent men, it's just as much as we all (and I mean all of us) are more than happy to take you home and do weird shit to you, we are not going to take home a girl that has seen more bell ends than weekends and introduce her to our parents and friends as our new girlfriend. You are perfectly entitled to embrace life and live it to the fullest, have as much no strings attached sex as you want, but don't turn around and play the 'woe is me I just want to find a nice guy' card when you've literally been through nearly every guy in town. Same goes for the guys, you can't cry about 'just want to find a nice girl' on Facebook, when you've happily bragged about banging everything with tits and a pulse to everyone in ear shot. Trust me when I tell you you did have a nice girl, I met her, she seemed pleasant and didn't come off as slutty or annoying, so maybe and I mean just maybe you shouldn't have got caught out getting tagged in pictures on Facebook – oh the old Facebook gotcha – of your finger banging the shit out of some random walking bag of Chlamydia.

One of my favourite people on the clubbing scene is my friend Dolly, this chick is the embodiment of cliché stripper, she gets naked for a living, binge drinks, does more bugle than a marching band and has probably ridden more dick than all the girls from Geordie Shore combined over all seasons and do you know why I like her? Because she is honest about it, she doesn't fuck a different guy every weekend and then start quoting Marilyn Monroe all over Facebook and asking why there are no decent men. She's honest and that is one thing I do respect in people – oh and before you ask, no we have never slept together.

Nights weren't all doom and gloom; there were some of the most entertaining and disgusting nights I've experienced working at that club. I can honestly say I have had every single bodily fluid on me whilst working and I mean every last one. If it can come out of a human being it has been on me. The one night that stands out was a Friday night one summer. A radio call goes off to the male toilets. Everyone is off like a fucking rocket, no one on our team liked to miss out on the chance for a scrap – after standing around looking at

ADDICTED TO THE LIFE

four walls and a sea of drunks for a couple of hours, you kind of hope for a fight, just to break up the monotony – we bundle through the cramped corridor and spill into the gents. The toilet attendant tells us there's some guy who's been in there a while. Noting exciting, so the boys all file back out the door and I'm left in there with Dan. Dan is the internal supervisor – that means it's his job to oversee the inside running of the club when it comes to the security - so it's my glorious job to manoeuvre whatever mess is awaiting me behind the cubicle door. I bang on the door and shout for the guy to come out. As usual there is no response. Dan hops up on the toilet in the cubicle next door and has a look over, "Seb the guys smashed and trying to knock out a wank." I tell Dan to fuck off and stop being a dick. I take a couple steps back from the door and prepare to kick it open. Again Dan tells me the guy is trying to knock out a wank. "Oh fuck off Danny!" I lean back, throw a kick into the door and it swings part open, I bundled inside and bear hug the guy up against the back cubicle wall. As I'm holding him up I can look into his eyes and he has this weird look about him. His eyes are glazed over, but he has an almost look of peace about him along with some half dopey grin. As I look at him and ask why the fuck he didn't open the door when told, Dan shouts over to me to look down. I look down and realise that this guys trousers and down around his ankles, then I notice his boxers are down by his ankles as well. Could this moment get any more fucking awkward? Yes it turns out it could. As I look up and scan the rest of him, I can't help but notice he has his cock in his hand. Oh great Dan wasn't lying, it appears this guy was actually trying to knock out a drunken wank. It takes a few moments, but I suddenly twig at exactly which direction he's got his cock pointed. I turn my head to the side and look down at my right arm. Oh my fucking God, there is jizz on my fucking arm, actual human jizz on my arm, his jizz on my arm, not mine, but his dirty fucking homemade nut mustard is coagulating on my fucking forearm and it's not a small amount, this fuckers been building that up for some time! I drag the guy out of the cubicle, through the toilets and through the fucking club, his pants and trousers still around his ankles, his cock still in hand and his jizz still running down my arm. I dump him outside on the front steps in front of Rudi, the head doorman. Rudi looks at me and asks what the fuck have I brought him out like that for?! "Look at my fucking arm Rudi. He's wanked on my fucking arm, look at it! Look at it!" Rudi bursts out laughing. I walked back inside and straight into the cleaners' area and started washing my arm with the bleach used to clean the floors. Not a fun day at the office.

This would not be my first time being disgusted by other people's bodily fluids or ablutions, but luckily the next time it wouldn't hit my arm...

One of the main things you learn whilst doing door work is how to spot when someone is full of shit. I don't mean customers; they're easy, because they are usually drunk and always full of shit. I mean the doormen that give it the big one and then bottle it at the last minute.

If you've ever been in a night club working as a bouncer then you'll probably be familiar with this scenario. I'm stood up on the top VIP balcony and a few of the girls from Wiggle have come in – that's a strip club – as they usually do and one of them who's a regular comes up to say hello. We chat for a bit as you do when you're working and after a little while in the club and a lot of drinks, she comes up again and decided to get very close

ADDICTED TO THE LIFE

whilst talking to me. One thing leads to another and she decides the best idea is to grind against me, purely for her amusement. Now this can and will inevitably lead to a certain outcome – much like spooning – yeah, you guessed it, I'm rocking a hard on, and it's not like I can just pop off and take care of it. Luckily for me the awkwardness of the situation ends due to a call on the radio, there's a fight on the dance floor. I charge off to get to the dance floor and more importantly the fight and pretty much hit a running spear on some kiddie. "BOOM!" Now whilst I've got him pinned down to the floor, I have for the time forgotten about my little mate being not so little. The guy starts mumbling and I tell him to speak up or shut up. He admits he's done wrong, but asks if I would mind not digging my radio into his back. I look down and tell him it's not my radio, I'm just really happy to be here. The kid fucking screams! I drag him up, walk him out the side door and then rearrange my hard on and wander back in to find the stripper and carry on our conversation – sometimes door work is really fun.

Back to my previous point about people being full of shit – like most guys I got distracted by boobs. Now I was known for banging anything that moved – I had found my rhythm in the club scene. If I wouldn't take the girl home, then there really did have to be something wrong with her. When I walked into V the other boys would greet me by clapping, this was an inside joke – kindly started by Scott - about me being so riddled with STDs' that I was the walking clap (unsurprisingly I am single.) So one night I and one of the other doormen Danny have been talking to a couple of strippers that are in the club and after work we head over to a late night spot for a few drinks and to relax. After a while one of the girls suggests we all go back to her place and have some group fun. I'm all over the idea. I have absolutely no problem teaming up with a mate to have sex with a couple girls at the same time. I'm perfectly secure in my manhood and understanding that having two hot chicks in bed is more fun that having one hot chic in bed. It gets down to the last minute and the other doorman backs out and busts the whole night for everyone. The next night at work I ask him why he didn't go through with it. He tells me that it was because he didn't want to risk catching anything as he had a Mrs. at home – this is not a valid excuse from him as he gladly fooled around with one of the strippers in the train toilet the week before. Well you could have worn a condom! He goes oh yeah and then quickly changes the subject..... Some guys are all show and no go!

There was a girl who was working at our sister club over Poole called Dundee's – I'll get to the glamour of working Poole at a later date – and she is a perfect example of going through the clubbing scene and coming out the other side, she is also the perfect example of the type of girls we dealt with back then. Cesca was by all accounts a nice girl, but she happened to have some sort of thing with Dan. Dan from what I know had slipped her one at some point – naughty naughty as he had a Mrs – and this particular night she ended up at the club. After we've closed down Dan asks me to do him a favour and go outside and get rid of her, so being the friend I am I went outside and got rid of her.

Now over the course of the next week or so we end up chatting and spending some time together, we went on a couple of dates and slept together a couple of times and unfortunately this was one of the times I got caught up with someone that I shouldn't have.

ADDICTED TO THE LIFE

This one incident taught me two very valuable things: firstly there are girls you fuck and there are girls you date, just like you don't get satellite TV for a portaloo, this was not a girl to date. Secondly when even I bag up, then you know this girl is a walking STD clinic. I believe now she is settled down with a fella and have a baby on the way, but back in the day she went through more bell ends than weekends, I have a lot of penis cousins with this one girl.

Penis cousins are if you and your mate have banged the same chic, then you are related through sex – aka penis cousins. I don't know what the female version of penis cousins is...Cooch cousins?

So I'd been at the club for almost a year, my reputation had already flourished as being known for violence and an absurd ability to handle huge quantities of drugs. A camera had been installed in the spiral staircase that was now known as Seb cam. This was after an incident where a guy goes through the double doors up the top of the stairs and out of camera shot, then appears a minute later in the reception area with his face covered in blood and his front teeth missing. I'm not saying I did anything untoward, but the guy was part of two guys kicking a guy in the head whilst he was on the floor and unable to adequately defend himself. I ran up and punched one guy in the face to nullify him and the other guy I brought out through the exit and downstairs in the most responsible manner I thought necessary at that time.

One incident that really solidified my ability to start a riot out of nowhere was what has now been lovingly referred to as the war on boat shoes. So we finished another boring student night and as part of the job we have to disperse people out the club and into the street, but the fun doesn't end there, no no no, we get to help move people down the road.

The reason we have to monitor and help control people outside of the venue is called a duty of care. Now you may not appreciate a doorman telling you to wind on down the road, but it is a part of our license and if you get injured in our 'area' then we have a legal responsibility to you. Trust me, we want to go home and get the fuck away as fast as possible and we have no desire to be anywhere nears you.

I'm outside V and I'm walking around with no real enthusiasm telling people to move on and mind out the way of the taxis and buses that are coming through. I tell one guy 'jump up on the pavement mate; you don't want to get hit by a bus.' Now his response is "I'm not dumb enough to get hit by a bus you fucking mug." Now I'll admit I was a little perturbed by his response, it did hurt my feelings a little and I wasn't about to take shit from someone wearing boat shoes, so I thought the best thing to do was to begin an exchange of dialogue and see why he was so aggressive.

I asked the cunt what the fuck his problem was and shoved him up on to the pavement – possibly saving his life – and for some reason he morphed into a lawyer. You can't touch me, that's assault and moved towards me. I explained that was not assault but a method of removing him from harm's way, I then called him an ungrateful prick and slapped him across his stupid fucking face. With that a large group of his friends coming running towards me.

ADDICTED TO THE LIFE

Ah fantastic. The boys come running off the steps of the club and a mass brawl erupts in the middle of the street. There were bodies being flung everywhere. Rob was spinning guys one after the other towards me and I was just thumping the little fuckers one after the other. Scott threw a kid through the newly erected fence and it slid all the way down to the bottom of the car park. After a good few minutes of group bonding the boys all wandered back into the club to write the incident report. You always have to make sure you get your paperwork done just in case. Needless to say everything ended up fine, Captain Boat shoes disappeared into the night with his band of skinny jean clad helpers. And the boys and I had a beer inside the club to relax after a stressful night.

The one thing that gets me and most doormen annoyed are the stupid fucking comments from managers. We get told when we hear a radio call and we have to respond to a situation somewhere in the club, we are to take our time and not bump into other customers as the club does not want to have to replace people's drinks if we knock them out of the way whilst responding to a radio call. Let me state clearly and directly to any manager that says or has said this to doorman – FUCK YOU – if we are responding to a call for a fight or violent incident, then we get there as fast as we fucking can. It takes one punch or kick to seriously injure or even kill someone. There have been numerous articles in the news about a kid being struck and then dying from undiagnosed head injuries or being left brain damaged after a fight in a club or in the street. I would rather spill a hundred drinks and pay for those than casually walk up to a fight and find a guy now dead from a shot that could have been avoided if we had gotten there sooner. And if you think I'm wrong, then fine. I ask any manager to walk up to the parents of a child who is now paralysed or brain damaged or even dead after an incident in their night club and tell those parents that although their child is dead, they didn't have to refund a couple of spilt vodka red bulls so it's okay. That is genuinely the level of pedantic bull shit that we have to listen to from most managers.

When people ask is it easier to deal with girls in clubs than guys, they always seem surprised when you say guys. It's very simple. If a guy is pissed or kicking off, then you just grab him and out he goes no more drama than that. You have to get rid of a girl and they suddenly go into sexual assault mode. You can't touch me I'm a girl. You're not allowed to touch me. WRONG. In the clubbing world much like in the real world, if you do something wrong and you need to be removed from somewhere then you are a genderless entity. Just like with the police, you can't stop a police man from arresting you because you're a girl and he's a guy. Your ass, as pretty as it is in your little hot pants is leaving. So we get a call to the female toilets, these are always awkward as you don't generally have a fight going on, it's normally some drunk bird who's thrown up on herself and that's just not fun. So me and the guys come through and see what's going on. Turns out my instincts were right! Scott, Dan and I are greeted by the female toilet attendant who has a girl passed out in the cubicles. We manage to get the door open and get a look at the scale of what we are dealing with. She is absolutely fucking wasted, sat on the toilet, knickers by her ankles and vomit down the front her and to top it off she has thrown up and passed out whilst having a shit! Guess who gets to help her up, yeah that would be me. So I very carefully get this girl up and moving, at this point we've wrapped her in her coat not because we care about her dignity, but I don't want to get covered in vomit and shit. We get her through the club and en route bump into her friends and she is now their responsibility.

ADDICTED TO THE LIFE

So I had been at V for almost a year and things were going pretty much as well as they could for me. Scott and I had formed a pretty good team especially when it came to picking up women. Scott was like a magnet for women. Being that he was built like an absolute freak of nature and covered in a near enough body suit of tattoos made him pretty eye catching and interesting to almost everyone, especially females. And the thing with girls is they don't go out on their own. So who was there to wingman with him? You guessed it, me.

One night we had been talking to a couple girls who worked at Walkabout that Scott knew. Well he knew one of them as I think she'd taken a ride on the Scott train before and her mate just so happened to be looking for a gentleman friend to fight off the cold of night with. They asked if Scott knew any single doorman or staff in the club and Scott apparently pointed to me on the other side of the club and the 'friend' took a walk round to get a look at me, went back to her friend and said I'd do. Scott asked if I was game – silly question as I would bang a ham sandwich if it looked at me right. They had told us to pick them up from the flats above Walkabout when we finished. You have never seen a street clearance completed so fast by doormen. We jumped in our respective cars and drove round to their flats and waited outside. You could see some shadowy figures looking out the windows of the club in our general direction. The doors to the side swung open and out came the girls, they waved each other goodbye and jumped in their allotted cars and off we went to cuddle and tell bed time stories.

The next morning after a tiring night of cuddling I asked who was watching us from the club windows. Jo my lady for the evening laughed and explained that when they had come back their door team had asked what they were doing and they explained they were going back to meet up with a couple of doormen from V. The door team there had said please tell us it's not Seb and Scott? Low and behold five minutes later mine and Scott's cars pulled up outside and they watched the two girls jump in. That was the last bit of fun I was going to be having at V.

One of the problems with night clubs you'll find is everyone knows everyone and you really can't get away with much. You'll go round and round in circles and without realising it everyone will know and undoubtedly be in your business.

Here's an example of how things get complicated. Now I was working at the club and spotted a regular chick that came in and then she popped up on my Facebook feed, so I added her, her name was Jaimie – you'll later know her as mini me. We get talking at the club the next week and that transpires into talking over Facebook. We get on ok as far as general chatting goes, so I ask her for a drink and she says yes. For whatever reason the next week she cancels. Later on I talk to her and she says she's just not interested in dating anyone – fair enough. We kept chatting and up getting on pretty well.

So a few weeks later she ends up getting in a relationship with a friend of mine Leigh – *Firstly I will not be referring to him by his (self appointed) nickname Legz as it does not in my mind do justice to who he is or what he is. There is nothing wrong with Leigh a part from*

ADDICTED TO THE LIFE

the fact he can't just be Leigh. He has to be this image he has in his mind and this is brought to you through buckets of bullshit. Claims to have been an ex marine, fired from V for putting someone in a coma, working for the yakuza in China, working for gangsters in Bournemouth, this imaginary facade of being some sort of feared bad ass. He's a bullshit artist and after the way he acted at Dave's funeral he's a disrespectful fucking punk! Don't like it? Not hard to find me. Pumped full of steroids and picking on people who were smaller than average. But every time someone said something back and called him on being punk he backed the fuck down and coward...Legz? Don't make me laugh more like Ovaries... – and for whatever reason it doesn't work out after a little while. Now as I said we get on well and still carried on chatting. The fact we're also normally seen out with the same group of people gets people asking if we're together. I always say no. Now the issue with the situation was that it was always fine for us to be out together, if she had a fella on the go or an interest then there was never an issue, but if I pulled or was not with the group because I was chatting to a girl, then there would always be an issue.

After months of back and forth we had a massive blow out one night. I happened to be getting on a girl in the club and one thing leads to another and there's an incident somewhere in the club between the girls. So now I've got a drunk and screaming Jaimie going mad at me for not coming with her when she wanted to leave, because I was "busy."

We ended up having a chat a few days later and squaring things away, but it did lead to some unpleasant conversations. I told her she only had an issue when she was single and I was busy with a girl. I had asked her out, she had said no then dated a mate of mine. I stated the fact that I had tried to get her to give it a go, but she had ended up dating another guy at the same time and that I was pretty much done with asking her out. She either had to ask me or we probably shouldn't be around each other anymore, because it just didn't work. Needless to say we didn't ever date and we don't really talk that much either and haven't done since then. *I do still like her as a friend, but it'll never be what it was.*

It was December and the club was rammed night in and night out. We had guest appearances from Danny Dyer all the way down to the cast of TOWIE (it had just gone on TV and was an absolute smash – fuck knows why?) I was working on position at the top of the stairs beside the DJ area, when all of a sudden I'm soaking wet! I look around and on the balcony just beside some bird is walking away with a bottle in her hand laughing. I walk up and ask her what the fuck her game is? She laughs and just tries to ignore me, so I tell to mind her fucking self and stop being dick. I walk back over to my position and carry on looking out over the crowd. Whack! Something catches me on the corner of my eye. I'm a little confused for a second and it takes a moment to gather myself. I look to my side to see what's happened. That same girl is laughing walking back to her table again. I look to the other side and on the floor is a full can of red bull. That bitch has just thrown a full can at my face. Needless to say I'm not happy. I begin to walk over to the table as a little bit of blood starts to run down from my eye. I grab the girl by the arm and tell her to get the fuck out! As I grab her the guy on the table with her stands up and moves to come towards me. I very kindly tell him to sit the fuck back down and he does. So I'm dragging this bitch by the arm and she's screaming at me to get Lee. Fuck off love you're not getting shit. We get to the top

ADDICTED TO THE LIFE

of the stairs and she starts to struggle and fighting me. I've had enough at this point and the other doorman who's meant to be working with me is just stood in his own world. The stairs are a bastard to bring someone down at the best of times. There is no safe way to do it (despite what the SIA say) and she is fucking clawing and thumping me, so fucks it. I throw her ass down them. She lands halfway down and as I walk down, she starts to threaten me and try to fight me. Easy fix, boom a swift kick and she slides the last few steps to the bottom. At this point every fucking doorman has now been alerted and coming running over. Everyone is bundling in and trying to grab her and me and I'm losing my fucking shit with people. I don't care what the fuck is happening you do not come in and start trying to man handle your team mates.

After the situation is calmed down and I've stopped yelling at everyone Karl comes over to explain the situation to me. Apparently the girl in question is the owners girlfriend and she has a habit when drunk or on drugs of throwing bottles at doormen for her own amusement. Low and behold she also happens to be Karl's best friend. Karl tells me that they are not going to report the incident, but he will get the girl to apologise for attempting to blind me for her own amusement. Fuck off Karl! I argue that it's okay for someone to assault a member of door staff, and because they're sucking and fucking the owner apparently it just takes a sorry and it's all good. I told Karl there and then you either remove her from the club or I'm going home. No doorman is expected to work in that situation. He offers to put me on the smoking area for the last three hours. Oh how kind, I get banished outside so she can carry on drinking and sniffing coke. No deal, get fucked, I'm off home.

I was called the next day by one of the guys from the door team and told Karl had written up statements, asked Lee and the other doormen to sign them in regards to the incident. Apparently he'd drafted some bullshit letter stating that his friend hadn't done anything and that I had attacked her for no reason. The guys refused to sign anything. Daryl one of the managers at the club and an old school friend went straight to the office to check out the CCTV footage, but unfortunately it was not clear on that part of the balcony, but he had attempted to have my back along with the rest of the boys and I'm very thankful for that. Surprise surprise the next day it would appear the cameras hadn't been working and there was now no footage of any of the incident at all, funny that?!

I got a call from the office about the incident and was spoken to by one of the directors, Marc. Marc told me it was sorted and that I was to have a couple days off from the club to let the air settle. Apparently Richard the owner had heard about the incident and banned his girlfriend from going in the club anymore. I gave it a few days and then that turned into a week and that turned into two weeks. Something wasn't adding up. Every time I called the office Marc was not available. Considering the guy spent all his time sat on his ass updating Facebook with boxing crap you would think he would be near a phone.

One night I got sick of waiting and decided to go have a drink. I was at the pub next to the club drinking with my brother and his friends and thought fuck it, I'll pop next door and say hello. I go in say hi to the guys and grab a beer at the upstairs bar. Low and behold Marc comes in to do some security for the clubs special guest that night. He makes no effort

COCAINE COMBAT

ADDICTED TO THE LIFE

to acknowledge my existence and I carry on having my drink. A few minutes later my friend Chris who is working at the time walks up and tells me that Marc has ordered me to be removed from the building. Are you having a fucking laugh? Chris tells me that I can hide downstairs and finish my drink as long as Mark doesn't see me. No, fuck off. If he wants me out, then he can come and fucking remove me. Chris is trying to be as diplomatic as he can. He's got his boss on one side wanting me gone and his mate who is now raging and refusing to leave on the other side. Not a fun place for any guy to be in, but he knows that quite frankly I don't fucking care about his position and the only way I'm going is if I decided to go on my own accord. Chris is also far too aware that if he or anyone else does physically try to move me I'll start a fucking riot then and there. Eventually, after a few minutes I calm down, and say I'll leave to save the boys any agro, but I'm walking out on my own, unescorted and only once I've finished my beer. Deal!

Few days later and I'm stood in the Gallery tattoo parlour owned by mate Jordan and as I look out I can see Marc sat at a table having a coffee with some little blonde bird at the cafe over the road. I ring his phone and watch him check the screen then cancel the call. I ring it again and he does the same. So I ring it a third time and this time he answers and tells me he can't talk he's in the office about to go into a very important meeting. I call the office and speak to Ross. Ross god bless him is the guy who manages the office and all the staff. He does all the work so Marc can sit in his chair wanking off over boxing memes. I tell him what's just happened and that I quit and don't ever contact me again.

The problem with some people is they can be as big as a house, tanked up on steroids and be the big man of the company, they can wield the power to hire and fire you as they please, they can stand behind a team of six or seven guys when the shit hits the fan and look the business, but really they're just a scared little boy, trying to fake everyone into thinking they're something special. Marc you're a gutless fucking coward and a joke. If you don't like what I've had to say about you, then feel free to message me or walk up to me any time you see me and we'll step round the back and you can put that ABA championship boxing pedigree you bullshit about to the test with me anytime. Just remember Seb plays fair, but Wimbo sometimes has a surprise up his sleeve just in case – insert winky face.

Suppose it's now time to look for a new place of employment, but whose going to hire a steroid infused, drug abusing lunatic with a negative reputation and overly enthusiastic fondness for violence?

ADDICTED TO THE LIFE

The Man With The Tattooed Face

There are some people you meet who just turn your way of thinking upside down. I was at Joe's tattoo parlour – that's Scott's brother Joe Munroe world re-known tattoo artist - when he showed me a video of a guy he knew through the tattoo community. The guys name was Jay Read and he seemed like a character from out of a Guy Ritchie movie. I watched a video that someone had made of Jay for a university project. The video didn't paint Jay in the best light, but it was interesting. Joe told me a bit more about him and I found some other videos of him on YouTube and after a couple of days I had an idea.

I sent Jay a message via Facebook about the idea of doing a film based on his life and some of the experiences he had been through. A few days later I got a message back from Jay who was interested in having a proper chat and seemed genuinely flattered by the idea that someone would be interested in documenting his life. So we arranged a day and I made the four hour trip up to Jays place in London.

I pulled up and was greeted by Jay. We met at what I think was his girlfriends parents house, which happened to be empty apart from us. Now all I had to go on was a series of small videos on YouTube and the exchange of a couple of messages via Facebook. Jay made quite the impression when you saw him. He had a full body suit of tattoos and that included his head and face, platinum capped teeth and a bit of a mixed London and Birmingham accent. I really didn't know what to expect when I got there, but he was by far one of the most welcoming people I have ever met. He seemed genuinely humbled by the fact I found what little I knew about his life film worthy – I will point out it took over four hours for him to offer me a cup of tea. Sorry Jay but your hosting skills aren't great.

We sat down in the lounge and just started chatting. He would ask me a few questions about my ideas and I would ask him general questions about his life and then respond with ideas of how they would possibly translate to the screen. At some point it just morphed into a conversation about everything and anything, we shared jokes and stories about women and embarrassing incidents. It evolved into the equivalent of two friends sat in a pub on a Sunday afternoon.

The one thing I learnt most from Jay - other than his awful beverage offering skills – was his ability to think and adapt to pretty much anything. He had a very distinctive and inspiring way of thinking. It was going through the initial idea of the film that the idea for this book began in essence. If you look on his Jilted Royalty website it has a section called bio, he has put a summary of his entire life leading up to his starting Jilted Royalty and one of the first things he mentions is his split personality disorder. When he told me about that in the opening part of our meeting it really resonated with me. This guy looked like he would kill you with his eyes, the videos I had seen would have you prepared to meet the very epitome of walking masculinity and machismo, but you got greeted by this open and honest and very well educated man, who had a real sense of self confidence. I hadn't ever had anyone talk openly about their mental health and some of the issues they suffered, let alone put it up on a

ADDICTED TO THE LIFE

web site for the world to see. That was the marking of someone who was truly comfortable in themselves.

Eventually his girlfriend came home from work. We had been chatting for about five hours without stopping. She happened to be a very successful alternative model, she had just been featured in a series of high profile magazines and music videos and was essentially the hottest ticket in town when it came to alternative modelling. She was just as welcoming and offered me a cup of tea. I had started that day with no real idea of what to expect and was ending it having tea and marmite on toast with the most famous alternative model on the planet and one of the most fascinating people I had ever met.

Jay owns one of the most successful clothing brands out there 'Jilted Royalty' and it's inspired a series of other companies and clothing brands to launch their own 'versions' based on his unique style. Sadly the film didn't materialise due to Jays heavy work load and near obsessive dedication to his clothing business. We did recently bump into each other at a tattoo convention and he was just as pleasant and humble as he was the years previously despite his now monstrous success and cult following.

Like they say, you never know who you're going to meet and how the smallest encounters can change so many things.

On a side note he was the first person to message me when I did my first stand up gig wishing me luck.

The problem with looking back is that you can realise what you were doing wrong and spot the problems, but you have absolutely no way of going back in time and fixing them. I used to think the way I did things was because that was the way I had seen things done before. You know with crap TV shows or those awful documentaries they make about the life of a doorman. I had this gut feeling that something was fundamentally wrong with me, but I had no idea what it was. I just accepted that this was the way things happened. I had had a shit end of the stick when it came to life for a bit and getting on the club scene had opened up some new doors and exposed me to a more interesting way of life.

That wasn't the case. I learned now that for a period of roughly three years I had suffered with depression. I had always thought that the reason I lashed out or went from 0 – 100 every time something happened was because I was either juiced up or that I just wanted to fight. Looking back I was not overly aggressive or lashing out because I liked to fight. It was because I was fucking terrified. I had severe anxiety and one of the symptoms associated with anxiety is at times and inability to control your temper. It's not really a bout of rage but a bout of despair. Feeling lost, overwhelmed, scare, and uneasy. You revert into your instincts natural state – just like when you corner a wild animal. The drugs gave me a false sense of understanding and it would have some very heavy consequences as time went on.

ADDICTED TO THE LIFE

Going Tropical

So I'm banging about sort of treading water trying to find something to do. I'm not working in the day time, all I did was meet Scott in the morning, and we would go to the gym and train and then go have a nandos. There wasn't really much else that interested me.

I had never really had an idea of what I wanted to do as a child, people would ask you at school what you want to be when you grow up and I would say I didn't know. I had never really been pointed towards anything with a particular purpose or set goal in mind. I had left school very underwhelmed with education and people in general – I had begun to use drugs more and more at that point – and just went into college as I had nothing else to do, but very quickly began no showing and failing classes.

When someone asked me the question 'if you had a million pounds what would you do?' Essentially whatever you answer is your career as it's what you would do if you had the ability and total freedom to do anything. My answer was 'nothing.' But that is not an option, not one that pays well anyway. So I did the only thing that made sense to me at that time and joined my friends in the venture of pharmaceutical distribution. That was my go to move for many years to come.

Luckily for me Scott had been fired from V a few weeks before I was. One of the directors had seen video footage of Scott on the front door talking with two girls and drinking coffee, looking a little too relaxed apparently and decided to bring Scott in for a talking to. Mr M spoke with Scott after his meeting with the other directors and told him he didn't see anything wrong with it, you're a young guy enjoying his work and told Scott he had no hard feelings towards him. Scott had decided that working for that company wasn't going well and left to find a new venture. I had taken a few weeks off to get away from the drama of door work, but money had started to run thin and I needed to find a new venue to work. As it happened Scott started working at the Kukui nightclub a club just across the square from V and they apparently needed another doorman. Scott spoke to the head door Matt and he said for me to come down and do a Thursday night. That was their student night and it got pretty busy.

My first shift I turned up, met the guys I'd be working with, got introduced to the manager and got told how it worked down there. Matt was pretty sound and was an old school bouncer; he'd been doing this shit for years. He told me the club could get a little fighty at times, but the management were cool as long as you didn't do anything out in the open in front of queuing customers as it was not the best look to see a doorman stoving in some kiddies as you're waiting to come in for a drink. I met the manager Ryan who luckily happened to be sound as fuck. The bar staff hated him, because he was a bastard to them, but he was absolutely golden with the door team, he had your back every time.

The door team was pretty sound, you had big Tomasz who was this massive former power lifter from Poland, and happened to be billed as the largest man in MMA at that time,

ADDICTED TO THE LIFE

Polish Matt, Polish Jacob who was another massive bodybuilder type, Nic who was a short, crazy, South African, Neil who had been doing the doors for years, Justin who I nicknamed 'The Face' as he was just so fucking pretty, he literally could get a girl pregnant just by looking at her, and of course Scott and Matt as I mentioned earlier.

The club had a small bar upstairs as you came through the door and to the left a stairway leading down to the main dance floor.

My first couple of shifts were pretty uneventful. One night things got a little heated between Jacob and some moron. Jacob brought a guy to me and told me to get him. I was stood at the bottom of the stairs next to the entrance to the dance floor and at the bottom of the stairs leading up to the club entrance. I told the guy to walk out. He asked what he had done and I said I don't know. I'm not there to run and check for you. Once you're outside, then we'll go and clarify why, until then just walk out and don't be a dick. Sadly this guy didn't take that advice. I'm trying to walk him upstairs and he starts shouting don't touch me! I'm not fucking touching him, I have one hand on the small of his back trying to guide him, and it's a standard move by every doorman to help move you forward that puts little to no pressure on someone. He turns round and starts to get in my face; he's got two friends with him. I'm guessing he thinks he's pretty tough – side note time: At this time I have a baseball sized hernia sticking out of my groin, my ability to wrestle with people is pretty limited and I'm in continuous pain, so I'm pretty easily wound up – wrong way of thinking! I grab his throat and pin him to the wall with my left hand (I'm right handed, so I kept that free in case I have to hit someone.) As I'm trying to tell him to calm down and just walk out he slaps me clean across the face. I lost my shit and just unloaded on him, it took moments and the guy was on the floor trying to crawl into the cloakroom to get away from me. I was relentless and had absolutely lost it, I was on top of him throwing hooks into his ribs and head and screaming incoherent rage at him. The girls at the reception at the top of the stairs had seen this and got Nic off the front door to come down. Nic had seen me and three guys all bundled at the bottom of the stairs and assumed I was in trouble. He leapt down the stairs and squared off with the other two guys. After a brief moment he realised the other guys weren't fighting and were screaming please get your doorman off our friend. He looked round, and I'm still on top of this guy pretty much slamming the cloak room door on him. Nic grabbed me off the guy and told me to go up stairs to the other bar and calm down. He then got the guys out of the club. Matt told me that the guy I'd been fighting with looked like he'd been in a car accident. He came up and asked me what happened, so I told him. Ryan came up from the office and chatted to me, he understood and said to me "you see all those people looking in through the big glass front of the club?" I nodded and he said well they've just seen you nearly kill someone. The advice he gave me was to next time do it where there aren't any customers waiting to come in. I apologised and told him next time I'll make sure I'm away from the entrance. Ryan knew fighting couldn't be avoided in a nightclub and he knew sometimes door staff, like the general public, will get a bit carried away. His concern was business. He knew I was going to be good to have around, if there were larger incidents, but he also knew that if I did that again and it affected business, then he was going to have to fire me. I understood that perfectly.

ADDICTED TO THE LIFE

As I mentioned I'm working with a baseball sized hernia. A hernia is when your abdominal wall tears and your intestines are sticking through and if left untreated this can cause death. The main problem is I'm a guy whose working at less than a hundred percent, I'm being told whilst I'm waiting for my surgery (which has an undetermined date) I'm supposed to be taking painkillers and not doing anything in the gym. Two problems: I'm a functioning drug addict and the one thing that helps keep me levelled out I'm not supposed to do. If you've ever taken steroids you will know it's incredibly hard to stop taking them. You see your body grow and change and then all of a sudden you're left looking like half the man you used to be. You're tormented by thoughts of weakness and insecurities when you look at your shrinking physique. I was stood outside the club when one of the girls, who were working at V at the time Stacey, came over with her friend Sara and they had a quick chat with me and one of the first things they said was "you've lost some size Seb." This type of stuff puts you even more on edge and aggressive. You get guys in the club who start giving it the mouth when you're trying to deal with a situation, because to them your just some average looking guy and what the fuck are you going to be able to do if they decided they don't want to leave. What was the only option in my mind on how to deal with this? Be so overly aggressive from the start that anyone who came into the club would know you were not to be fucked with. How did I do this? I couldn't train so taking steroids to bulk up was pointless, but taking much larger quantities of testosterone would keep my strength roughly where it should be and made me super aggressive all the time. Scott was the ultimate visual deterrent and me; well I was the team psycho. Fuck asking you to put the bottle down or stop kicking off at people, boom! I just pounced like a wild animal and unloaded with everything I had no matter what the situation was.

I'm not trying to sound like an idiot or a loser when I say this, but I pretty much lived for my weekends working on the doors. My life was a mess, I was living with Scott and he would see me come home in the most spun out, incoherent states night after night. The only times I was levelled out was when I was working, and even then I was on a tremendous amount of uppers to keep me going through my shift. I loved my nights with the boys; they were my family and my safety net. When you're work revolves around being part of a team that has to watch each other's back and care as much about your safety as they do theirs, why wouldn't you feel happy when you're with them?

Although the team was different the bond between the guys was exactly the same. Only this time there weren't any shady behind the scenes bullshit and drama to deal with. The only time the disabled toilets were locked was when one of the boys was having a quickie during the shift (MATT.)

The club was new to me, but everything else was the same as it had been at my old place. Girls came up and flirted and twirled their hair, and then just when they thought you were eating out of the palm of their hand, they asked if you could get them free drinks. That's when we would say no and they would then walk away. So fucking transparent it was sickening. But on the plus side they seemed younger and prettier than the girls I had seen before.

ADDICTED TO THE LIFE

I'll give you an example of something that really pisses doormen off and that's when random girls with a vague connection to you think they can get royal treatment. As I said Scott worked at the club also. Scott has a brother Joe, Joe just so happens to be a world renowned tattoo artist. Joe had literally begun dating a girl called Charlene for about two days at most. I'm stood on the front door and this group of girls walks up, shows me their Id's and then asks if I know which one Scott is? I tell them he would be the massive guy covered in tattoos. They ask if I can call him to the front door, so I do. Scott walks up and has no fucking clue who these girls are. They ask him for free entry. Scott asks why and the girls say "our friend Charlene goes out with your brother Joe." Scott asks what the fuck that has to do with them getting free entry from him. For some reason the girls seemed confused that a guy wouldn't give free entry to a group of girls he'd never met, who happen to be friends with the girl he barely knows, who happens to have been bouncing up and down on his brothers tattooed cock for the last 24hrs. Funny that. A couple hours later I threw one of them out for being a goby twat.

Finally I've had my surgery and I'm instructed by the doctors not to do anything physical for the next 6 weeks and absolutely no door work for the same amount of time. I had taken a job at a personal training company for the last month or so, we sold PT courses to people, the job was boring, but it gave me something to do during the day time. It was the morning after my surgery and I was laid out on the sofa, I was pretty strung out on valiums and wasn't too coherent most of the time. My phone rings and I struggle up and answer it, it's my day job. My boss had called me to tell me the company had decided to fire me. I asked why and he said he didn't know, they just didn't want me back. I said they had to give me a reason and eventually he told me. A couple of clients had been walking around the office and heard me talking about the stair incident that got me fired from V and they had apparently made a comment about the type of staff the company had to the owner.

The next day I told Scott what happened and we decided to drive down to the offices and have a word. I came limping through the office door and sat at the sofa and demanded to talk with the owner. The office manager came over to me and said the owner wasn't here and I was to leave. I told him that I wasn't leaving and that I knew the owner was here, because we blocked his car in. When I said we, he looked at me and looked confused, then Scott stepped in through the doorway essentially blocking the only way out.

A few minutes later the floor manager came back to us and said the owner was not coming down. I said that's his decision, but I'm not leaving until I get a clear answer as to why I was fired. The floor manager then told me that I had made a racial comment and it had been reported, I asked what was the comment, who did I say it to, who overheard it and who reported it, and why was I not called into a meeting as they are now saying I'm a racist. He told me he couldn't tell me the answer to any of my questions and that if I checked my contract then I would see I was under probation and could be terminated at any time without reason or explanation. There was an uneasy acknowledgement and I knew they were full of shit, but I also knew I couldn't do anything about it. Scott helped me up off the sofa and I slowly walked out, sadly by some poor accident I lost my footing as I walked past the owners

ADDICTED TO THE LIFE

Lamborghini and tried to steady myself on the car door, unfortunately I didn't do a good job and ripped the wing mirror off.

Well after having a week off I realised two things: I could now move off the sofa without shouting for help and more importantly my ass could not afford to not be at work. So back we went. Matt moved me onto the front door for a few shifts as I was next to useless if a fight broke out, but after a bit of time I realised I had slow but okay mobility and I could just punch people until help arrived instead of trying to wrestle with them. So back into the basement I went, back amongst the thongs and body odour.

Now I was still running on an insane amount of drugs. One night big Jacob came up to me and offered me a clenbuterol to help perk me up before the shift started. I asked if he had anymore. He looked at me like I was out of my mind. This guy is easily 6ft4 and 19st and he takes one and that sends him to Mars. When he then watched me take a further three clenbuterol to add to the one he had given me and then pop two T5s and wash it down with a red bull his eyes just widened with disbelief. He actually asked Scott once how I wasn't dead. Little did he know I'd already overdosed months before and just carried on my life exactly the same as before – not my smartest move.

So an overdose, let me break it down for you, I'm assuming not everyone has had one. An overdose can be used to cover a different range of reactions to drugs. If you get so spun out from a long bender involving drugs, drink and you get so dehydrated you end up on a drip in hospital, then they classify that as an overdose. Needing your heart restarted is classified as an overdose. As you can see it can be a bit of a broad spectrum – *mine were more on the 'fuck I believe my heart is about to explode' side of things.*

I hadn't intended to overdose, I hadn't intended to die, and I hadn't intended not to overdose or not die. I was doing Russian roulette with a variety of pills. I remember feeling something, I couldn't put my finger on what it was, but I didn't like it. At the weekends during the club I was fine. I was using to keep me awake and able. When I was away from that, I was using to cope with everyday life or not cope depending on your view point. I'm not really a particularly religious person, but when you're on your own and you feel like voicing things in your head out loud, I guess if you pose it as a question to God, then you sound a little less insane than if you were talking to yourself. I asked why? Why am I like this, what the fuck was this feeling I couldn't shake? I didn't get an answer back. I figured I'd play with some pills, if I was meant to stick around, then I'd wake up the next day and I guess I would carry on with my life and try to figure out what the purpose of it was. If I didn't wake up, then at least I wouldn't have this feeling hanging over me anymore.

The next day I woke up and things had never felt worse, I went to the bathroom, my head was spinning, I vomited some blood, crawled back to my room and took a couple of valium to slow things down. I woke up properly a little while later and although I felt rough as fuck, I carried on with my day.

I have never been a fan of therapy or counselling. It was not that I thought it meant you were weak or inferior. It was that I just didn't think it worked. I was recommended by my

ADDICTED TO THE LIFE

mum to talk to someone – someone who was an actual professional and paid to give an 'expert' opinion or insight into my mind... I'm not being rude, but you really don't want to tap into my mind. It's a rough fucking lace at times. I went and sat down in front of this guy. It was in one of the most depressing fucking buildings you could imagine. If you weren't suicidal before you fucking would be sitting in that shit hole. The guy asked me what I wanted I sat and thought for a minute... I just want to be happy again, like before all of this. Like when I was a kid. I was happy just happy existing like everyone else... He instantly responded with 'I can't make you a kid again!'Not what I had asked nor was it what I wanted – who the fuck wants to go through puberty again? – So fuck him, fuck therapy, and fuck everybody.

There are a few incidents that stand out in my mind during my time working at Kukui. This could be because they were really interesting compared to the usual day to day grind we endure or it could be most likely due to my memory being extensively affected by a decade plus of drug abuse.

I'm looking out over the usual siege of teeny boppers we have in on student night, all blending into each other with their cut and copy haircuts and baggy t shirts they wear in an ironic statement to counteract the sight of what appears to be their pre-pubescent, undeveloped physiques. I'm on the slightly raised seating area directly as you come down into the main dance room, leaning against the column and generally floating about in the murky depths of depravity that at the time was my mind, when BOOM! Scott is suddenly wrestling two guys across the dance floor. I say 'wrestling' he was quite easily holding one in each arm. Bless them they looked like a couple of salmon being pulled out of the water by a fucking grizzly bear!

I set off like a fucking rocket into the crowd and sent Jaeger bombs and WKDs absolutely everywhere and just as I get to a few feet from where Scott is I yell 'got one' and speared a kiddie straight out of his arm. Scott loves to tell people that my yell was the most feminine sounding call he's ever heard in his life. However, I distinctly remember it being at the height of manliness! Like a lion roar! Now I've tackled this stupid kid to the floor and I'm now on top bearing down on him like he's the new boy at boarding school and I'm the head boy. I tell him not to be a dick and stop struggling or I really will start to hurt him. He ignores my considerate warnings and decides to try and bite my left arm which is under his left arm pit and across his shoulders/neck area. There is only option now (there were in hindsight probably a couple of other options) but to start giving him a few gentle digs to encourage him around to my way of thinking. I post off his back a little bit to create some room and allow him to get a more stable base on his hands and knees (we are on a soaking wet dance floor bundled in amongst a load of sweaty dancing teenagers.) Once he has got himself to a more stable point, I use the space I had created to throw a couple of right hands underneath his right arm and torso and up into his face...crack...crack. Two decent shots and he's now a little more cooperative, so I hoist him up and turn around to a rather disgruntled looking Scott whom states that cheeky fucker took a swing at me and then proceeds strike the kid in the face with his shovel like hand.

ADDICTED TO THE LIFE

The kid goes out like a fucking light in my arms, so I shake him round a bit and he comes to.... BOOM...another shot from Scott and the kid goes out a-fucking-gain. I shake him back awake again and this time I manage to manoeuvre him out of the club and away from the anvil hands of the bromance.

In this next section as you read it you'll probably think at points I may have over reacted or have done things that were clearly not necessary? I ask you keep an open mind and then wait for my explanation at the end. Then feel free to make your opinion based on all the factors.

The call goes through! Fuck it we're off! A code red is called on the front door; this means that they want every doorman there as fast as they can as something big is happening. I burst through the doors out into the street and straight into some kiddie, fuck knows what the issue was, but when it's a code red you come in hard and take out every fucker insight.

I'm a few yards further out from the club than everyone else; Matt is behind me looking the other way, so he can't see what's behind him. It's my responsibility to stop him getting cheap shotted from behind and vice versa. As I look up to my side some kiddie is taking a run up behind Matt to try and get a shot in. Foolish move kid, I step my side a threw my right hand as hard as I could and this guy is running forward on to it – if you have ever watched any MMA you'll see guys running forward or stepping into a punch that doesn't look that hard, but the impact of all your weight moving forward onto even the slightest punch can turn a light jab into a lights out moment – WHACK! I remember that this kid didn't fall backwards or into the air in a spectacular movie style fashion, but rather on impact his legs just seemed to crumple from underneath him and he just collapsed on the spot and then just slid backwards.

I am screaming at this kid don't fucking move! He starts to sit up, WHACK! I scream at the kid again to stay the fuck down. Matt looks up just in time to see this kid sit up again WHACK! This time the kid says I'm down I'm down and he stays there.

I cannot really remember much of the incident other than that particular interaction, but it highlights a key point. As a doorman or bouncer or whatever it is you call it the most important factor of the job is always the same! You watch each other's back! The reason doormen become so close and build some really intense friendships with each other is for exactly that reason.

People come up to me a hundred times a fucking night and tell me they're going to sit the door supervisor course and get their badge. They tell me that they might not be very big or capable in a fight, but they are a good talker and teams need that nowadays. Now to a certain extent I believe in what they say, but talking or not the guys you're working with, the guys who are stepping in the way of bottles, knives, punches, kicks and whatever else for you, need to know that you are able and willing to return the favour. If you can't do that, then this job is not for you. In my eyes you are a danger and liability and if I get hurt, because you were hesitant or bottled it, then when I'm done with whatever's just happened I am going to rip you to fucking shreds and so will anybody else.

ADDICTED TO THE LIFE

Managers will tell you, you can talk anybody down and criticise you for being physical. This is because they are looking at the club through eyes with a business tint. Their main objective is to make money and collect their bonuses at the end of the year. They now have to do the SIA course as part of the licensing act to be able to be a pub or club manager. They often think because they have sat the bullshit four day courses, that they are a fucking expert on how you should do your job. Sadly they are mostly fucking idiots who think they know everything (AMY.)

I'll give anybody a chance and numerous times this has been my downfall. When it comes to door work it can take a bit of time for a guy who has just started to find his feet and get the ropes. There is however no excuse for repeated pussying!

My boss at the time was a guy called black Nigel. Everyone called him black Nigel because he was black and his name was Nigel. Nigel was about 5ft6 at best and 8ft fucking wide, the guy had gorilla power. Every time he shook your hand you braced yourself as it felt like a fucking vice grip crushing your fingers. He didn't do it on purpose, or to be some tough guy he just had gorilla like power. He was one of the most straight to the point guys I've worked for and I always appreciated that. Too many people try to mince words and dance around the issue, not Nigel.

Nigel had contracts for various clubs. When we were short they would send an extra body over from a less busy club to help out. We were absolutely rammed one night and Matt told me we were getting a guy over from Klute to help out.

I had never met the guy before, but the reviews were not favourable (doormen talk to each other a lot.) We're short and need the cover, so what are you going to do? Just bring the guy in and see for yourself. Dan (another Dan) turned up and for the most he looked the part, he was gym goer, had some size to him and seemed keen. So I put him downstairs and explained the basics, just watch the crowd and radio if you need anything.

I come back and he's stood with his back to the crowd, talking to the group of girls on the table. So I walk up and tap him on the shoulder and explain you can talk to the girls, but you have to be watching the dance floor. I go on my internal wander and come back to find him with his back to the dance floor talking to the girls again. Again I go over and tell him. I go for another wander to check on things and when I come back, low and behold he's doing it a fucking again! This time I walk up to Matt and tell him to send the guy home, he's fucking useless and does not listen. So Matt calls the guy up and sends him home.

I'm speaking to my mate Lee during the week and tell him about Dan and he tells me the guy worked at V for a bit, but they got rid of him because he would go missing whenever a fight got called. They found him twice hiding or 'monitoring' the furthest fucking corner he could find away from the fight. Lee told me the guy just kept making excuses that he couldn't hear the call on his radio or he didn't see anybody running to the incidents.

The weekend draws near again and it is time to go to work. The club is fucking rammed again (must have been the welcoming and friendly door team drawing in the crowds)

ADDICTED TO THE LIFE

and again we are short. Who do we get told is being sent over? It's super Dan! He turns up and I put him down on the steps leading up to the smoking area and 12ft from the main bar. He can only look forward at people, so no need to worry about him not seeing anything this week.

At some point in the night we get a call on the radio for the main bar. I'm upstairs so come running down and find two of the team wrestling two guys out the smoking area and Dan was looking like a lost puppy a few feet away.

After the commotion has settled and everyone is back on position where they were before I ask one of the guys what happened and why Dan was stood doing fuck all when he was the nearest guy to incident and therefore should have been the first one in. He has no idea, when he got there the two guys were fighting and Dan was on the floor.

Later I get pulled over by one of the bar man. He tells me about the fight. Apparently Dan had seen these two guys suddenly erupt into a fist fight. They just so happened to be stood next to a dwarf (they like to party just as much as the rest of us.) Dan looks at the two guys fighting and then at the dwarf stood directly next to them, but not actually involved in any way, shape or form according to the member of bar staff. Dan decides to jump and tackle the dwarf. He apparently attempts to tackle the dwarf (not anyone involved in the fight, but a fucking bystander) and completely fucks it up. He lands on the floor face down with his arms creating a circle around the dwarf. The dwarf looks down and just steps over his arms and out of the way of the two gentlemen who are still fighting. It was the bar supervisor whom made the radio call.

He is a nice enough guy, but unfortunately the decision is Dan is out. He is a liability, dangerous, useless and a fucking pussy when it comes to confrontation.

Now this section of the book would not be right if it did not have a special mention of one of the good friends I have been fortunate enough to make over my time as bouncer or doorman or attitude adjuster or whatever you would like to call it.... Justin Moore aka 'The Face.'

There are some good looking guys who work the doors and there are some guys who genuinely have to graft to get a girls attention. Justin was by far in a different league of good looking bastards. The guy just has something about him that made every girl who came into close proximity of him suddenly weak at the knees. The guy could literally get a girl pregnant by just looking at her. God knows what he was like between the sheets, but I imagine he's no slouch – insert winky face.

It just so happened to be that he was also a handy bastard to have by your side if and when the shit hit the proverbial fan. To this day we are still good friends and it was me that adorned him with the nickname 'The Face.'

One time at the club we had a fill in DJ as our usual guy was away and this guy seemed to get really annoyed with people asking him for songs – I figured that was part and parcel of being a club DJ – and at the end of the night we had cleared everybody out apart

ADDICTED TO THE LIFE

from two customers who were just putting their drinks down. All of sudden the DJ walks out from behind his booth and punches one guy clean in the face. Justin and I now have to wrestle with these guys and get them out; my guy backs off and gets out the way. Justin is on top of guy trying to hold him down when this guy pokes his head up and bits down on Justin's chest. I come over and hit the guy in the ribs a couple times to get him to release his vice like bite on Justin and we bundle the guy outside. Needless to say the DJ was never brought back and Justin had teeth marks for about two weeks.

One of the things you start to notice when you are working is that certain songs trigger certain reactions from the crowd. Every good DJ can read a crowd and get a feel for what type of music they seem to be responding to. Well every time our DJ Simon played Black and Yellow it would, for some unknown reason make a fight break out. I have no idea why this happened, but it always did when the song came on. As soon as the first beat kicked in I always got that adrenaline rush before you walk out to a fight.

My most memorable hallmark during my time at Kukui was the fact for the last couple of months I would always finish my Saturday shift an hour early to slide off with a particular female. She was affectionately known by the guys at the club as subway girl.

She was and still is my friend Charlie. Charlie and I had been on a date quite a while before I started my time with the guys at Kukui and we had had a 'romantic encounter' a night prior to our dalliance at the club.

During a two month period we would hook up at the club – side note, she would come in with her friends and they would ask her if she could get me to get them in, she would always say no, because she didn't want to be rude or take advantage. I still have respect for her for that - she would come in on the Saturday and I would get to leave early (whilst being paid until the end) to take Charlie home. Every time she would say she was hungry and every time I would have to swing by subway and get her something to eat. And every fucking time she would drop this subway on my car floor when we went round a particular corner. EVERY FUCKING TIME! The guys at the car valeting place started giving me a discount because I was in there having the car cleaned on a weekly basis.

One evening as I was trying to sneak out the side door early and avoid Ryan the manager – as it was a pretty sure bet he didn't appreciate paying a doorman to leave early and have sex – he suddenly stuck his head out the main door as I was trying to sneak off. Ryan asked what was going on and Matt without hesitation said "Seb's off to bang that girl." Ryan not missing a beat shouted out "give her one for the lads!" All the boys erupted with cheers. I laughed and shouted back "I'll think of you." Charlie did not laugh!

She has been going out with an old friend of mine for the last couple of years and I wish them both the best. They make a lovely couple and are very suited to each other.

The only other eventful occasion with a female during that time that's worth mentioning was with my friend Sophie. We had slept together before for a period when her and her then boyfriend had stopped seeing each other for a couple of months and we decided

ADDICTED TO THE LIFE

that being sex buddies would be helpful. I do remember her saying to her dad she was meeting me and when he asked how she knew me, she said through college. I get the feeling he was expecting a 17/18 year old boy to turn up to see his barely legal daughter and not a 24 year old bouncer.

Sophie called me one night saying she had had an argument with the fella and he walked out saying it was over. She called me for a chat and I said to come over, she turned up with a bottle of wine and I think you can see where the story heads from here. The only awkward moment was a few hours later when her phone went off and it was her ex fella saying he was headed to the flat to pick up his things, only problem was that she was in my bed. I've never had a girl leave so quickly, it was like a smoke trail behind her. To this day we still get on well and she loves retelling the story about how she broke my dick.

Suppose as I've mentioned it I might as well tell you. So 90% of guys out there have snapped the banjo chord, it happens when you go in a bit too dry, especially when a girl climbs on top without being wet enough to self lube your cock. Well one night we're going at it and we've rolled over for a bit, I'm on my back and Sophie is busy making out with little big man whilst take a five minute breather. All of a sudden she yanks on my sack and this lightning bolt of pain seers through my balls. I manage to finish up, but when I look down at the tissues they are covered in blood and cum. I feel quite ill at this sight and get a little light headed.

I go to the clinic to find out what's wrong as it's not like one of the injuries I've had before during sex and I am informed that I've torn the epididimus – the tube that carries spunk from your sack through your cock and out upon ejaculation. His advice no sex or wanking for two months as it'll keep hurting the tear and keep bleeding. No sex for two months doable, but no wanking either, doc you're asking the impossible!

As I mentioned earlier I was on some form of drug related substance all of the time. At work it was T5 and clenbuterol. For about three weeks we had a relief manager called Zeb whilst Ryan was on holiday. Zeb was pretty relaxed when it came to the club. He would only be there a short time and therefore didn't interfere with the door team and what we got up to.

One night Zeb walked up to me after I had taken my usual work cocktail and expressed his concern over the fact my eyes looked 'mental' and it was clear I had taken something. And it looked bad when you compared it to the rest of the door team. I told him not to worry and I would sort it out. So I went round the club and gave every doorman in there a T5. Zeb came out of the office after a little while, looked around the club and saw every single doorman bug eyed, sweating and tapping their feet to the music. We looked more like a collection raving, high Vis beacons rather a team of security professionals. I told Zeb I had fixed the problem and he just stood speechless looking at me. I did the only thing I could think of and offered him a T5. He just walked away repeating "that isn't what I meant by fix it."

That night Scott and I decided we could get a better feel of what was going on if we just stood in the middle of the dance floor and whilst there why not have a little boogie. Well someone told Matt the head door and he came down to find the two of us in the middle of the dance floor happily shaking it with a group of three girls. Matt walked over, looked at Scott and myself, then at the three girls and decided he would even out the numbers. The three of us spent the rest of the night dancing with these three girls. Now that is what a team does for each other!

Living with Scott was always an interesting time. I lived in a bungalow that his brother owned and lived in with us; we had another roommate Ben, who was either asleep or off his nut. Joe would have people in all day at his tattoo studio – he had built a full studio in the back garden. There wasn't much to do during the day so I would go in and get tattooed by his apprentice Jack, work out, and go to nandos or to my nans for tea and cake. Scott had a girlfriend at the time, but when she was at work we would go out and he would come with me to my nans and occasionally to pick up bits and bobs.

Joe always said he enjoyed having us at the house, because it meant he had his own built insecurity team or as he called us 'his steroid, monkey, doormen army.' Joe was also my morning aid when it came to getting up on a Friday after I had worked the night before. I would come home around 4am and have work at 10am. I would always take a valium to knock me out and Joe would essentially get up at 9am and come into my room, physically sit me up out of bed and then come check on me after twenty minutes to make sure I hadn't passed out again.

One of the odd things that came out of working at Kukui was my seemingly gifted ability to perform stand up comedy. On the Thursday night when we had insane waiting times on the front door for entry I would sometimes help Matt and Nic with the crowd.

A particular night I was stood at the front of the queue telling people how long the wait was. A couple of girls at the front (who later became my friends India and Roxy) asked what they were meant to do whilst they waited. Nic piped up and told them that I had been to a performing arts college. So they asked what I could do. I told them I did a stand up comedy unite as part of my course and proceeded to do a full ten minute set there on the front step to the awaiting crowd of clubbers.

The story of a stand up performing bouncer at this club got round and so on Thursdays when the queue was long and people had to wait, I would do little routines and keep them amused. See we're not all thump and dump, we have other skills. I had just started doing actual shows for the first time and the guys from Joe's tattoo parlour and the club would come and watch. They were a very different looking audience to what the other comedians had become accustomed to. At one gig a comedian came on after me and half way through his act said he couldn't finish the rest of it. He had material about guys on steroids and tattoos and took one look at my table of fans and decided he didn't want to say anything. The funny thing was my table said for him to do it, it would be fun, but he was just too nervous to do it.

The problem I seemed to generate was a burdening reputation as a guy who really just didn't seem to give a fuck. I took every drug going, loved it when the fights kicked off and

ADDICTED TO THE LIFE

would more or less sleep with anything with tits and a pulse – I guess maybe I was making up for the years I felt I missed out on with all the drama I went through in my younger years - this came to be a slight problem after two remarks were made. One of our bar staff Emily, sweet girl, quite artsy and really pretty, got shit faced on her birthday in the club. By the end when we were closing she had lost all her friends and was barely able to function. I offered her a lift home and she accepted. IT WAS JUST A LIFT HOME! I got her address to her dads and helped her out the club. As I was walking out with her Ryan came up and said Seb remember she's drunk, don't try anything. I would like to take the opportunity to mention that I know how to explain the difference between a drunken fumble and rape – not that anything was going to or did happen, I am at times a gentleman. Anyway, I drove her back to her dads and got her inside, safe and sound without a mark on her and her dignity and pussy intact.

Zeb had been an interesting guy to work with, he was very concerned when it came to what the boys and I would take on shift, but at the start of each shift we had an arrangement. I would leave three little packages in my jacket pocket in the cloakroom and at some point in the night a small fairy would replace those packets with money. Shortly after Ryan came back from his holiday things went array for the boys. We had been accused of being overly abusive and racist to the international students on the Fridays when they had foreign student night.

The ironic twist was that the defence they had was: well look at the door team. Firstly I'll just point out that I fully admit to being overly aggressive or abusive at times with people, but never once was it based on their race or anything like that. If I'm calling you a cunt, it's because you are being a cunt and for no other reason!

Our 'racist' door team consisted of Matt who was full English, Neil who was mixed race, Nic who was South African, Polish Jacob – enough said, Scott who was Greek, the bromance Scott who was English, but his mum was married to an Arab, Big Tomasz who was Polish, Justin who was English and myself who is half English half Spanish, all working for a guy called black Nigel. We were the most ethnically diverse door team you could fucking find. Needless to say about 90% of the team left as the issue went back and forth and it was just more aggravation than it was worth.

So where to go now?

COCAINE COMBAT

ADDICTED TO THE LIFE

Same Old Shit

Once again I'm left without a place of employment. And much like with women, sometimes you foolishly go back to someone you left for a very good reason, but hey we're only human.

I happened to be joking around with Rudi – the old head door when I was at V – who just so happened to now be the head door at a pub, the Mary Shelley in town. For some reason I don't quite recall he had left or been forced to move from V. He worked for the same door company, just at another venue. Anyway we got talking and I joked that I would come back and work for him, but only if they gave me X amount of hours and start and finish times of my choosing. Low and behold he asked me to come back and work for him – I think he missed the feel of V and having me around would remind of the fun we had.

Pubs work differently than night clubs. Obviously they open earlier and close earlier but you get a lot more foot traffic as people use them for pre drinks. They get right up to the point of being smashed and then bail out just in time to still look mildly sober enough to get past the security at which ever club they want to get into.

From the offset I knew this was not going to be a long term fix for me. The place just did not feel natural to me. I was and am very much a night club guy. Some people prefer working clubs, others pubs, others up market wine bars, we all have a certain preference.

My time at the Shelley did lead to two incidents that still stay firmly planted in my mind.

The first was the night Marc came to cover for us as we were a doorman short. This is one of the directors of the company and the guy you'll remember (if you read this thoroughly so far) I did not have the best feelings towards. Marc turns up and stands out at the front of the club on his phone for twenty minutes just pissing about doing whatever.

Now Marc is as I mentioned is one of the directors of the company and therefore was to be talked to with a certain level of respect, ha fuck off! The second Marc arrived I was on him and just digging away at him. When he turned up he asked so what's the deal here then? Before anyone could respond I was on him, "fucking hell Marc, I haven't got time to baby step you through it. You should know this by now. Fucking hell the office has sent us another guy who doesn't know what he's doing!" He turned up without an ear piece and I went straight in on him about not being prepared for work.

Marc spent the entire night stood outside about 6ft from the front door, eyes glued to his phone and then left early. There was absolutely no point in him having even come. If that's the level of cover you get, then don't even bother. The thing that got me was he didn't even try to talk to me. He didn't pull me to one side and just try to clear the air a little bit. And when I went in on him and just took the piss, he didn't even think to pull me over then and say I know you and me don't get a long, but you do have to respect the fact I'm your

ADDICTED TO THE LIFE

boss. There was absolutely nothing from him. The moment he saw me he tried to act like I wasn't there – foolish! – He had and still has absolutely no minerals (balls for those of you not up with the lingo.)

We still haven't spoken to this day. I don't know if he genuinely dislikes me, is afraid of confronting me, doesn't think I'm worthy of his response or if because for a few weeks I was banging a girl he was apparently seeing? I don't know, but the guy just tries to pretend he doesn't see me whenever we happen to be in the same place.

I always try to get to work a little early. It's not to kiss up or make a good impression, it's so I can have a fag and question the staff or managers on what bullshit I'm going to have to expect. This next night was no exception.

I turn up about fifteen minutes early and come to be greeted at the front door by Ravi and a guy who we can safely describe as shit faced drunk. The guy is trying to convince Ravi that he is okay – he is not okay – and should be allowed in to have another drink. It is 7:45pm and this guy looks like he should be staggering out of a strip club at 5am. He asks how he can prove he is sober enough to come in. Side note – never ask a doorman what you can do to prove how sober you are. We will try and think of the most bizarre and/or embarrassing things we can think of for you to do.

Ravi tells the guy if he can hop the length of the security railings, then he can come back in. Now the security railings are about 15ft long and I'll admit I don't have the most coordination at times and would probably wobble a bit. This guy is shit faced, but he accepts the challenge and is game to win the opportunity for another pint of Marston's smooth.

The man steadies himself and his nerves at the bottom of the railings and begins to focus on the task that lies before him. He takes a deep breath in, goes onto one foot and makes his first jump. He goes up into the air with grace and elegance and lands on with all the balance of a hippo on a parachute jump. BOOM he crashes into the barriers, stumbling over them and taking all of them out and two people who have stopped to watch the spectacle. He ends up rolling into the street and lying on his back, but still protesting that he should be allowed in.

That may not have seemed that entertaining to you, but what follows next for us was pure magic. The guy has begrudgingly accepted his fate with us and moved on down the road. He gets to the bottom end of the pub and crosses over the street to the parade of shops. He is still in full view of us on the front door and like responsible door staff we are still keeping an eye on him, just in case he wanders into traffic or something.

It would appear that he still felt he could have made it to the end of the barriers, because for some reason (I'm guessing drunken logic) he decides to have another go outside this random shop. He jumps and goes head first into the Barrettes shoe shop window, he lands in a heap face down on the floor outside, but the force of his head hitting the window has triggered the store alarm as it thinks someone is trying to break in.

COCAINE COMBAT

ADDICTED TO THE LIFE

As Ravi and I are in hysterics at the front door, a police car comes flying around the corner with the lights flashing and pulls up swiftly at the front of Barrettes. The police expecting to find some daring raid in progress are instead met by a half conscious drunk lying at their feet. They scan the scene and pretty swiftly access that this guy is not a master criminal or one of the great train robbers who is looking to get back in the game, but another shit faced moron. The police come over to Ravi and I and ask if we recognise the guy and if he came out of our venue. Ravi and I look at each other and declare we have no idea who he is or where he has come from.

Whilst briefly at the Shelley I also ended up doing a couple of nights back at V. I had walked past at the under 18s night and they mentioned they were short a guy that night. They had a new manager called Andy who knew exactly who I was and started chatting to me. He asked if I would cover, and I said it wasn't a problem if they were okay with it. I was also still going in there drinking on Mondays with some of the guys.

That night I helped out and had an uneventful night, so they asked me cover the following Monday student night. Now on the Saturday we removed a guy from the Shelley who had been harassing and touching women in the bar and when we threw him out he argued with us for ages – don't argue with us. It just means we will remember you more and more and that is not a good thing.

One of the nights I was in there drinking there was incident with a couple of guys. As Taz and I were coming down the stairs these two guys went for a mate of ours, so Taz instinctively swung, clocked one of the guys and as his mate came over the top I hit him. That was the end of it.

A few days later this guy comes up to the Mary Shelly (the guy I clocked whilst on the night out) and starts saying it was Lloyd that hit him, Lloyd tells him he wasn't even there, but if he wants an issue they can have one, they guy does fuck all and wanders off into the night. Apparently sometime later, someone gave him my name and he was going around looking for me. I posted a Facebook message up saying where to find me and if he wants to make an issue, then just pop on by.

Monday rolls around and I'm working in V club and this guy comes up to say you got an issue with my mate? I look up and this kid stood at the top of the stairs giving his best gangster pose. I say what's the problem then? He walks down and says I hit him the other night, I say yeah could be me and what? He says to meet him outside at 2am and we'll settle it. I tell him I finish at 3am and I'll happily meet him in the car park over the road.

Sometime later a girl comes up to me and reports that a guy in a red t-shirt has been rude and grabbed at her. I ask her to point him out to me and she points out the guy from Saturday night at the Shelley. I go to get one of the other doormen and ask if he wants to help me get rid of the guy. Just so happens to be my mate Bowler. He says nah he can't be bothered and so I go to find the guy again and remove him.

ADDICTED TO THE LIFE

I bring the guy to the reception area and tell him what's happened and that he is to leave. He argues with me and says I can't make him go. Ha foolish boy. I tell him to either walk out or I'll throw his ass out – there is nothing more annoying than some groping idiot who thinks he's the shit – and it won't be pleasant.

The guy turns to walk away from me and back into the club. I grab his arm and belt and march him towards the front door and start picking up a bit of speed in the process. As I come towards the glass doors about 8ft within the club doorway, Chris comes running towards me saying "no, no, no, no, no, no, no." I twist my hips and launch the guy as hard as I can out the glass doors and he just glides off the ground and through the doorway. Unfortunately what Chris was trying to warn me was that two police officers happened to be standing outside the front door.

The guy lands in amongst the barricades and right at the feet of the officers. As I turn to walk back in all you can hear on the radio is "Seb to the front door." I may be in a little bit of bother.

The officers break out the hand cuffs and whack them on and moved me up against the wall of the club and ask me to explain what happened. I tell them and say he tried to elbow me as he was leaving and that's why I had to move him forward with some force.

As I'm stood there, the wannabe gangster comes walking out the club and starts heading off. I shout I thought you wanted to meet later and wave my cuffs at him. He looks at me and tries to pretend he doesn't see me and walks off into the night. Just another fucking mouth piece with no balls.

They go and talk to the guy for a bit and tell me that he said if I apologise then he'll leave it be. I walk over to the guy and say so apparently you want an apology. He starts to get mouthy, so I just start calling him every name I can really quietly, so no one else can hear. The guy takes a step towards me and I call out to the police officer that he is being aggressive towards me. I remind the officer that they have handcuffed me and I am unable to defend myself if he attacks me. The officer comes over and the guy starts to mouth off to them. So they let the cuffs off me and take him away for being abusive.

I have to wait in the cloakroom until the end of the night as apparently I can't be trusted. At the end of the night I am walked to my car by 6 other doormen and informed I am banned from ever entering the premises again.

I had been at the Shelley for a month at best when I got a message from Polish Tomasz. Polish Tomasz was a fucking man mountain, a former power lifter who weighed in at 30st and had an extensive colourful past mixing with some of the less savoury characters in Poland. He was also a very caring father and a professional MMA fighter. He was now running the door at Klute, a night club and sushi bar on the other side of town and he was looking for door staff. From what I understand the brief from the owner was that he wanted the meanest and most handy door team he could get....Off to Klute we go and this is the year shit gets very different for me (but that's for the next story.)

COCAINE COMBAT

ADDICTED TO THE LIFE

I did have an offer from Chilli White a club in town to go and work for them. They were offering five nights a week and about 30hrs. That would be enough for me to live on; I was a man of simple needs, drugs and food mainly.

Unfortunately this job was gone before it even started. I was on a night out on Wednesday with some friends. One being Jaimie, she was referred to as 'mini me' and I was referred to by her as 'big me'. So we're in Chilli Whites and a guy comes over and starts hassling our group. He is told very politely to fuck off and he does. Later like every smart guy, he decides to come back and give the girls some more grief. Now Jaimie is small and sweet looking, but after a few drinks she can go psycho pretty quick – hence mini me – and she is not shy about telling this guy to fuck and try to physically move him herself.

The guys eventually leave the club and since our party buzz is fading we decide to find somewhere else to drink. As we're walking down the strip the guys appear again and a standoff ensues between Mossy and one of the guys. Now Nick Moss aka Mossy will state it was just a chat and the guy wasn't doing anything. I maintain he moved his hand in an aggressive manner towards Mossy face and I instinctively hit the guy. The problem with that was it was in front of another club door team, on the corner near police cars and in front of the guy who was supposed to be offering me a job. Needless to say I had to run through town dodging police and got a message from the guy at Chilli Whites saying not to start work there next week.

ADDICTED TO THE LIFE

Shit is about to get real interesting on every level

I really don't know where to even start with this section. I get the feeling it is going to jump around a lot, so be prepared and try and keep up.

I was on absolutely everything I could fucking find. My drug abuse was not abuse in my eyes, it was a necessity to function and deal with everyday life. I was on valiums to sleep, T5s to get me through the day, cocaine and weed were stable parts of my life. I'll try and put it into a clearer understanding for you. I wake up and to counteract the drowsy feeling of the valiums I would reach into my little box and grab whatever pills I could find, sometimes they were T5, sometimes they were clenbuterol and sometimes they were more valium. So then I would have to take even more of the uppers or do a very big bump of cocaine at varying points throughout the day to keep myself awake. Sometimes I would just inject a large amount of testosterone with the mindset that would kick in and jump start my day.

I had managed to get myself a day job as a plain clothes security guard at a major department store in town. The main reason being is that two of my friends worked there and when a vacancy came up they told me to apply and recommended me for the job. I also found a new night club to work at called Klute.

Before I even got to Klute people who I had never worked with had already heard about me. My love of drugs was known by everyone, more than my work on the doors, but the extent of it people always took as hearsay. An example of this was after a night out I was talking to my now good friend Jordan Miller (whom I met whilst working at Klute.) I told him that the night before I had been out for a couple of quiet drinks with my mate (who will remain anonymous because he doesn't want his mum to know he occasionally was a naughty boy) and gone through a half ounce between the two of us. I told him it was mainly me and that I think I had done about 8 grams in the ¾ hours we were out.

The next night Jordan happened to see my drinking partner from that night and asked him if I had really done (what in his mind was an inconceivable amount of coke on my own in that space of time) the 8 grams. My mate looked at him and said no. He stated he did about 4 grams that night and the other 10 or 12 had been done by me. My mate told me that Jordan just looked at him and stated how the fuck was I alive. Truth is that was nothing. I would go and go until the supply was completely run out. I watched a film with Jonny Depp in, I can't remember what it was called, but in it his character (based on a real life person) does 10 grams in 10 minutes just to see if he could do it. Challenge accepted. I was sat at home bored with my shoe box of cocaine and thought I'd give it a try. I did about 7 grams in 5 minutes and then I don't remember anything else. I'm still alive, and that is all I can tell you. To state my memory from years of varying forms of abuse is patchy is an understatement.

So I start at Klute and over the course of the first evening get to know the guys I'm working with. Every fucking one of them is a professional MMA fighter. Except Stefan who

ADDICTED TO THE LIFE

just so happened to be a former Olympic wrestler. So it's professional MMA fighters, an Olympian and a stand up comedian – that would be me.

The layout of Klute was for the most part very annoying. You had a main entrance that lead straight up a flight of stairs to the first floor dance floor and carried on up to the second floor restaurant/dance floor/smoking area. As you went into the main dance floor you had a row of seating directly to your left that went all the way along, a completely circular bar and behind that were the VIP booths. At the end of the room directly opposite the entrance was a DJ booth and a double door leading to a back stairway.

I remember a fight kicked off on the dance floor and every one of the guys piled in. It was right up against the double doors leading to the private stairway and next to the DJ booth. We scuffled with this large group and bundled bodies out down the non camera stairwell at the back and left them all outside. Outside whilst people are still kicking off and giving it the 'lucky you're working or I'd kill you speech,' I notice Damo (one of the doormen) is not outside with us. I know he was involved in the incident, but he's not down here. I went back up into the club and found Damo with a front headlock on a guy bent over and up against a wall. I casually walked up and asked him what was going on. Damo said the guy was being a dick, wouldn't leave and had tried to fight him, so he locked him up. I did the only sensible thing I could think of. I walked behind the kid, reached down, grabbed his ball and then Damo and I lead him out the back by his face and balls. Problem solved!

The club was owned by Izzy and Turkish John. I cannot even begin to describe either of these guys in a way that would do them justice! Izzy was a former professional rugby player who had made millions setting up rugby schools throughout China or Japan, but had come to England after pretty much mauling a guy in a bar when he made an unflattering comment to his wife – his wife just so happened to be a former miss world or miss whatever country she was from (I never met her so I don't know.)

Turkish John was nuts, in the nicest possible way, he was nuts. He had no idea how to deal with people or any real business skills. He lectured us on various things that were of no use. He constantly yelled at us about people fighting in the club and doing excessive amounts of drugs, yet it was his little gangs of cronies and friends that were doing the drugs and constantly fighting with people.

Let me give you an example of how his people management skills worked. One night there was an incident with the Turks – his gang of friends that came in – it had ended in a near riot between door staff and them, everyone had spilled into the street and neither side was backing down. John being the sound and thoughtful employer he was, tried to get Matt the head doorman at the time to calm down the situation, and whilst talking to Matt, didn't warn him that one of his Turkish friends was sneaking up behind him with a knife. Luckily for Matt, Jessie a friend of ours whom just so happened to be out that night jumped in the way and took the knife intended for Matt's back to the top of his head. That is what we dealt with on a nightly basis.

ADDICTED TO THE LIFE

Now as I said at the same as working at Klute I was also now working at a department store and had been promoted to the security manager –oh so glamorous. So 3 nights a week we dealt with crazed cocaine fuelled drunks and employers and in the day time I put on a suit and was a responsible human being (all whilst lit up on drugs.)

Whilst working at Klute I became good friends with Jordan (who I mentioned earlier) and Dom aka Dom 'the dominator' Clark (current IFC middleweight champion.) The two of them have helped me out in varying ways tremendously over the last few years. While working with Jordan one night, he told me he had left his old MMA gym and was setting up his own training centre at a gym in Parkstone – just up the road from Bournemouth. We got to chatting and he asked if I had thought about giving it a try. It had never really occurred to me, but I had become a little bored with the gym. After a few years of just lifting weights day in day out you get a little bored. I figured what would be the harm in just doing some training. MMA was becoming the new in thing and everyone and their Nan was now claiming to be a cage fighter!

At the early part of my job at the department store I began seeing a girl called Amy. She was the best friend of my mate Lloyds ex fiancée and we were at a house party at Lloyds one night and we all got talking in the kitchen.

One of the guys had said to Amy if she wanted to meet a good guy then she should sleep with me. I had somehow built up a reputation as a sort of Good Luck Chuck – it's a film – character as all the girls I had recently slept with had then gone on to either lose weight, get better jobs or meet really nice guys. Amy very kindly laughed and said she would never ever have sex with me. Three weeks later we went on our first date and about a week after that we slept together – You're a woman of your word Amy *insert winky face.* Things didn't really work out and we just became good friends.

The ending of my dalliance with Amy just so happened to translate at the exact same time I had begun seeing a girl from work. And I don't mean she happened to come by the club every weekend and we'd hook up - she worked at the department store part time and was at the university studying - Well it was more the case that I was trying to go on dates with her- she was hesitant and over a couple of months was making me prove that I was interested in more than just a random hook up. Smart girl. Her name was Charlotte.

I was still a fully functioning addict, but I was open about everything with her from the start. I told all the stuff I had been involved in, all the bad stuff. I held absolutely nothing back and she accepted me for who was and who I had been. After about 2 or 3 months she gave in and we had our first date. It was all kept quiet, mainly because people love to get involved and give you their input when you never fucking asked for it!

We had a quiet date at my house just watching a DVD in the afternoon before she had to go to work. She told her parents she was working early and I picked her up from town and we headed to mine. We spent nearly two hours in pretty much silence watching a comedy DVD and at the end I leant in and kissed her, she was a bit surprised. When I dropped her off

ADDICTED TO THE LIFE

at work, she asked "what happens now as we work at the same place?" I told her it didn't matter to me and so we began dating. Keeping it all very quiet as people just love to interfere.

I got a message on Facebook one morning from Richard Carr – you remember I mentioned him earlier, he owned V – who apparently was not happy about some comments I had made on a status about not being allowed in his clubs anymore. We had a quick exchange and then arranged to have a meeting at the Mary Shelly just across the road from the department store I was working at.

It was all very civil. I walked in and he bought me a drink and then asked what my problem was. I explained the situation and we came to an agreement. I would keep from mouthing off on Facebook for a month and he would meet me again and see about letting me back in the clubs. We met a few weeks later having kept me end of the deal and he honoured his end of the arrangement. The funny thing was we actually got on really well after that. He was so used to having people just cower in front of him, that when I mouthed back I think he was genuinely quite impressed. We bumped into each other a few times since and have always had a very friendly exchange.

The problem is everyone thinks that you deal with everyone in the same way. That's just not the case, some people respond to subtly and some people only respond to a dick slap to the face, You just have to know who it is you're dealing with.

Klute had started to turn out to be quite fun. I was having a fucking ball during my time there. The managers Jack and Jonny V were on point. They backed us as best they could and knew how to keep us motivated when John would act like a fucking idiot towards us. Even had some old faces join the team – Matt and Justin aka 'The Face' from Kukui turned up to work there.

The team was an interesting mix. Everyone got on well and generally had a good crack. It was fun to come to work again. But my God was that place just filled with drama, drugs and aggravation on a daily basis!

I was in the office at work (my day job) one day and my boss Eddie comes in and says Karen the store director doesn't think we – aka the guys who worked with me doing the store security should be working at the night clubs as well as at the store. Before Eddie can say anything else I say that's fine, but we're all quitting. He looks at me in shock and as if I'm throwing a tantrum, I simply explain that at the moment I get 13phr at the club and the hours I do are about half of my day job and as I'm paid cash, the money works out more than I get from my day job. So if we're picking jobs, then I'm going with the money and that's at the club. Needless to say they dropped the idea of making us choose.

Christmas party story: So it's the stores Christmas party and of course everyone who works there is invited, this means an occasion for me and the boys to wear our big boy clothes and look dapper for the night. It is more importantly a night to see who will get in the most trouble. The party is in full flow and me and the boys are in full swing, I've already ended up hitting on one of the girls from menswear – I was dating Amy at the time which is

ADDICTED TO THE LIFE

not a good move on my part – and we decide that we should carry on drinking in town where the atmosphere is going to be a bit more lively. Karen the store manager is somewhat smashed and we decide we should bring her with us to the club. Lloyd calls a couple of taxis and we tell Eddie our boss that we are going and that Bowler may kidnap Karen for a laugh. Eddie finds this funny and thinks it's a joke, until he sees Bowler with Karen over his shoulder dive into the taxi and speed off. Lloyd, Mossy and I follow in another taxi and we all end up in Walkabout. Now I don't make the best decisions when drunk or drinking. I have literally been in Walkabout 5 minutes and I ended up pulling some girl off the perfume counter and right as I'm doing this in walks the girl from menswear is really not happy at this sight.

The night in Walkabout gets even more awkward as Karen is absolutely smashed and telling Lloyd and myself how her husband lives in Manchester and she gets lonely. Queue me hiding in the smoking area for the remainder of the night. As I decide to leave I jump in a taxi and on the way pass Bowler and Karen who are stood in the taxi rank, I say stood, Bowler is stood and Karen is slumped against him having thrown up down his shirt.

We get to work the next morning to find out the aftermath of what happened when we left. Apparently Bowler got one of the girls from work had got Karen back to a hotel and they had stayed there. The girl had crashed in the room with Karen and Bowler had slept in his car. He came up to the room in the morning to check the girls were ok and as Karen woke up he was stood at the end of the bed and for some reason blurted out "I did not sleep with you."

Needless to say Karen decided to take a job with another store back near her husband in Manchester.

Izzy was the owner of Klute and John's business partner - and also a different breed of human being, the likes of which I have never come across. When Izzy was on one and I mean on one for days straight, there was no way to predict what was he was going to do. There were nights when we would open up and he would just flip out and throw out whatever customers came through the door. You would stand there with people screaming and arguing with you and demanding you do something and you would just have to reply with "he's the owner. It's up to him what he does." Other nights Izzy would turn up perfectly fine and when he was like that he was absolutely on point! The guy ran a club better than most of the managers and owners I've seen. The thing with Izzy that you always respected was that he never went against the door team. He backed everything you did and wouldn't give you shit for no reason or just to make him look big in front of people.

The opposite of this was John. The guy lived to throw his weight around. Now doormen as you've seen in clubs have ear pieces in. This enables us to communicate with each other. Normally the managers will have one (if it's a big club) so you can call them to deal with specific things.

Radios are a fairly simple piece of equipment to use. You hold the button down and speak into the little microphone bit as clearly as you can. You'll see the old pros cup their hand around it drown out any excess noise from the club- insert winky face.

COCAINE COMBAT

ADDICTED TO THE LIFE

John decided he would use a radio and for an entire shift he just yelled incoherent babble down it. When you hear someone yelling your first instinct is that it is a fight, so you look around and start darting around the club trying to find what is going on. It just caused added drama. At some point in the night John was saying something down the radio that no one could understand. Apparently he was trying to get the attention of South African Nic (another face from Kukui) and Nic was not responding. So John thought the best thing for him to do was walk up to Nic and berates him in front of people...foolish!

Nic very kindly asks John to step into the doorway out of other people's view, so they can talk without interruption. Nic very kindly explains that if John ever does that to him again regardless of him being the owner, that he will beat the shit out of him. John stopped using a radio after that.

In the beginning the club would be open four or five nights a week. The week days were pretty quiet as you had competition from other clubs who already had nights set up. Any club that tries to launch a new night against an already established club night is in for an uphill struggle. You see hundreds of kids who think because they like a certain type of music, well then everybody else will do to. All you get is them, some of their friends and a very empty club.

The only guys I have seen who have really managed to nail the event scene in Bournemouth are the guys at Cocoloco. They started with one night and just worked at it for years and years, and now they do very very well from it.

The only guy who hands down, delivers without fail every time is a friend of mine Ilker. I met him working the doors and the guy knows everybody. He was the go to guy in Ibiza for years and would just annihilate the competition. Then he turned his hand to Bournemouth. He is a very useful guy to know.

I got on really well with Jack at club (he was one of the managers at Klute and then the sole manager); we shared a couple of awkward moments together. I'll give you a quick flashback story from one of my earlier shifts:

So it's a Tuesday night and I'm on a night off. I'm at home having a good time with the girl I'm seeing (Remember I was briefly seeing a girl called Amy before I started my relationship with Charlotte.) Anyway I'm in the middle of something – essentially Amy's legs- and my phone goes off. I lift my head from the task at hand and scan over to my phone and see it's the manager ringing me. I let it go and go back to what I was doing. The phone goes again and again its Jack from the club calling me. Amy being a team player chucks me my phone and I answer it.

Jack begins with some small talk and asks how my evening is going. I tell him that I am currently faced down in the bird and he is on speaker phone on her stomach. He laughs, calls me a pervert and asks if there is a chance I can come in and work. Apparently the club looks like it might get busy and there are only two guys working and John won't leave until someone else comes in. I tell him if they pay me for a full night then yeah I will. He says

ADDICTED TO THE LIFE

great and says how long will I be? I say I'll leave in about ten minutes, immediately Amy yells he'll need twenty minutes and winks at me. We are still good friends to this day. Some people don't work out in a dating sense, but if you're lucky you'll find yourself a new friend to laugh about with.

One Thursday night (student night) we are absolutely rammed. The throngs of drunken teeny boppers with their in trend top knots and skin tight trousers are bouncing around like fucking mad. The booths are packed out and everyone in them thinks they're a fucking celebrity.

I'm going to take a moment to help you out here. You can spend all the money in the world on a booth in a club. It does not make you untouchable or a celebrity and it sure as shit does not mean we won't absolutely rag the shit out of you for acting like a dick. I'll give you my best example of this: Back when we were at V and Scott is called to the VIP booths and I follow up a few moments later. When I arrive Scott literally throws a kid at me and says to get rid of him. I don't ask why, I just grab the kid and it's time to leave. The guy is arguing with me as we go down the spiral staircase and grabs hold of the banister and refuses to let go. He just keeps saying I know Steve, I know Steve (Steve is the manager.) I don't care and tell him let go of the banister or I'll break your fucking arm. He tells me I wouldn't dare! So I lift my right arm and drive down the point of my elbow right into his forearm. There's a pop type sound and he lets go screaming and clutching his arm.

If you get a doorman to the point where he is telling you he will happily maim you, because you're that annoying, then do as he fucking says. Some of them may be bluffing, but some of us will not think twice about it

As I said before the club is busy and we are all just waiting for the inevitable. It happens. Some fucking idiot has got into an argument over whatever and punched a kid in the face. As I go to deal with the situation, the kid turns to his left and tries to run around our circular bar, he head butts a random guy in the face to cause another distraction and ends up on the other side having a wrestle with Jordan. Jordan is more than capable of dealing with this dickhead, but I'm amped up and fuck it one in all in.

We bundle the kid through the double doors into the private stairwell. Jordan is balanced on the edge of the landing – if he falls backwards, then he is taking a tumble head first down a flight of concrete stairs – so I do what needs to be done and just start hitting this kid in the body, a few body shots and knee to his rib cage to put the little fucker down. I won't say what Jordan was doing as his body was off camera and why get him in possible trouble. Needless to say kid winds up at the bottom of the stair well. Now his friends have come through the double doors. I don't know what they thought would happen, if they thought they would step in and save their mate and deck a couple of doormen. After about a millisecond these two guys suddenly realised that stood in front of them are two doorman who are literally shaking, with veins popping out of their necks and who are not in the mood to fuck around, then behind them is now stood Matt and one of the other guys (I forget who.) Wisely they asked if they could leave quietly with their mate.

ADDICTED TO THE LIFE

Low and behold the second they're outside and there are now loads of people around they suddenly have all the fucking balls in the world.

Unsurprisingly when that kid got home and his mummy asked what happened he told her a gang of massive doormen had jumped him for absolutely no reason and beaten him half to death. Fucking lying pussy.

The incident got reported and police asked for CCTV footage from the club. I go down to Klute and meet Jack to review the footage. I'm not worried as it all happened in the stair well with no camera, so it would just be his word against mine.

Jack sets up the cameras and then gets a phone call, so he walks off and leaves me with the footage. The video plays and all seemed okay, until we get to the stair well. Some fucker has opened the doors during the incident and the camera from the end of the bar picks up the whole thing absolutely beautifully! I'll give Azon security systems credit; they provide a very clear picture with their systems.

I'm sat on the stool and all I can think is shit. This is not good and I'm in serious fucking trouble here! The picture provides a view of a very large doorman just thumping the shit out of some teeny bopper in a seemingly unprovoked fashion, but you and I know that's not the story – the police however may take a different view?

Jack comes down to the CCTV area and asks me how it looks and I tell him it looks fucking bad. He watches the footage and just repeats the words "oh fuck" over and over for about thirty seconds.

He immediately jumps on the phone to the clubs security company – you see we were paid directly by the club cash in hand, but the club used to pay another company to use their name on all the licensing paperwork. So if something happened at the club, then that company would need to be informed immediately – and I rung the only person I trusted in that situation Jordan Mooney. Jordan ran a security company, a tattoo parlour and several other businesses. He was a stand up guy, because even if you didn't work for him, he would happily give you legal advice and if need be put you in touch with a firm of solicitors. One of his guys was arrested on the job for whatever reason and by the time the guy got to the police station, Jordan had two solicitors waiting for him and paid the bill for him too. You don't get bosses who look after their guys like that anywhere!

I got my legal advice and Jack came back down with a list of things that I had to do as instructed by the other security company.

The security company Klute were using were trying to just cover their back in case some backlash hit them due to my incident. They did their best to try and make it look and sound like they were doing me a favour, but it was so transparent it was unreal. I got my legal advice from Jordan Mooney –the owner of Vanguard security and the tattoo parlour I mentioned earlier in the book – Jordan always helped out any one that asked. It didn't matter if you worked for him or not. The guy was a solid diamond.

ADDICTED TO THE LIFE

I knew their only objective was to limit the backlash on the club and I would inevitably be the fall guy!

I worked another shift for Klute that night and it turned about to be a real peach. There was an incident in one of the booths and I ran over and grabbed some guy who was punching someone. I have him in a bear hug from behind and he's fallen onto the sofa in front, so my arms are trapped under him and he's trapped under me. I can't reach my radio and am stuck waiting for someone else to see it and come over. I look to my right and a girl who is sat on the seating across the table casually stands up, picks up a full glass of whatever the fuck she's been drinking and throws it as hard as she can. I'm assuming she is aiming at the guy I'm currently stuck on, but it would appear she has had a few drinks and her aim is not great. The glass nails me right in the eye and slices my eyebrow open, there is blood pissing out of my right eyebrow all over the guy I'm holding. The girl just says sorry and casually sits back down and carries on drinking!

Finally one of the boys sees what's going on and comes over help me and we manoeuvre the guy down the stairs and out the club. Jack is screaming what have I done?! I tell him don't worry it's my blood and start filling out some paper work. Jack tells me to go inside as a doorman covered in blood is not a good look for the customers waiting to come in. I go upstairs and get the girl who has glassed me in the face and bring her to the front door. I tell Roy to keep her there until I come back.

Jack cleans me up inside the hall way and shoves some Vaseline into my eyebrow to hold everything in place. I walk back outside and the girl is gone. I ask Roy where the fuck she is and he tells me he told her to go and that she wouldn't be allowed back in again. Are you fucking kidding me?! I ask him if he remembers what she looks like and if he got her details? He says she was average with brown hair. Someone better call Sherlock Holmes and tell him he's out of a job.

After several minutes of me shouting at Jack about what a bullshit stupid move that was I calm down and walk back out to the front door. I am met by the girls' friend who comes up to talk to me. She apologises for her friend and finishes by saying and this is verbatim "in her defence she has had a very bad day." Well that makes it all fucking right then doesn't it.

The icing on the cake was a couple of days after this not only did the club let me go and the police filing charges against me, but I was supposed to be meeting Charlottes parents for the first time.

So a few days later and Charlotte and I are meant to be going on our second date. I drive up to her house on some estate over in Verwood, which is a little bit like a maze and I eventually find it. As I walk up to the front door Charlotte suddenly opens it and screams out. She was coming to help find me as she had seen me drive past the house a couple of times trying to find it, but I had got there just in time. I walk through the door and say hello to Charlottes mum. Let me put this into perspective for you: Charlotte is at the arts university, but she is completing an A-Level course, so she is seventeen (and a half.) Now I imagine her

ADDICTED TO THE LIFE

parents were expecting her to bring home a nice young man from the university and she turns up with a 25 year old bouncer, covered in tattoos and currently sporting a vagina over his right eye. I give her mum full respect for even having me in her house, let alone sitting down and having a cup of tea and trying to get to know me.

I think that may be a contender for most awkward parent meeting ever. Especially when she asked me about the night club, and I had to say I have just left the club as I've got a legal issue that has come up – not the best of first impressions.

ADDICTED TO THE LIFE

GBH is That A New Cocktail?

This chapter is a link between the previous chapter and the next. As my court case started at Klute, but ended at my next club, this seemed like the best way.

So the police have come to pay me a visit or more accurately summoned me to the station to do a formal interview over the incident involving the dickhead at Klute.

Here is how it broke down: the kid and his mum have reported the incident to the police, they've come to the club to investigate, taken one look at footage in the stairway and decided to charge me with GBH.

I get summoned to the police station to give a statement. I arrived at the station, told the receptionist I was here to see officer whoever it was and took a seat in the reception area. I was called up and brought through to the interview room. To say I was feeling a little uneasy about the situation would have been an understatement!

The charge sergeant was not a fan of doormen and he made that abundantly clear from the very start. I was asked if I wanted to wait for my representation, but I declined and said I would call my solicitor when I felt I the need to.

I explained my version of events and why I had dealt with the situation in the way I had. I was questioned as we went along, and at the end of it the officer instructed me that I would be going to court and charges would be brought against for GBH.

Now as much as I knew this dickhead had deserved everything that happened to him and I could reasonably argue my justifications for it, it still didn't stop my parents from being absolutely torn up about the whole situation.

Over the next couple of weeks I am going in and out of the station to go over statements, be updated on what's happening, and also to generally check I hadn't fled the country.

After one particularly fun interview I was informed that there was an option being put forward to me and that I could avoid some lengthy court hearing. I thought brilliant, finally they have seen through the bullshit and we can clear it all up and forget the matter. I was very naive it would appear. The option was more of an offer. I could plea to a lower a charge of assault, get a 3 month sentence probably do 6-8 weeks and be out, pay compensation to the kid and lose my SIA license.

This was not an option I was willing to take, but I had to get another opinion. My mates told me to tell them to fuck off, but when the other option is gambling on a not guilty verdict on a GBH charge that could lead to me being sentenced to 2.5 years and serving 15 months I was starting to think that offer wasn't too bad.

ADDICTED TO THE LIFE

I spoke to my dad and let him know the severity of the situation and he didn't know what to do. All he was thinking that whether it was a few weeks or a few months he was looking at losing his youngest son to her majesties pleasure.

I can't really explain how the situation makes you feel. Everyone tells you not to worry and just to carry on your day as normal, but you walk around feeling like you're on a time limit. Why make plans for a summer holiday when you may not be here, your mate invites you out for his birthday celebration next month, but you may not be here. You're looking at your bills and outstanding debts and wondering why you should bother paying them. It is just a constant pain in the back of your head without any rest bite.

The worst feeling is for your family. Every time you speak to your mum or dad it is the only thing they are thinking about, it is a continuous, unrelenting pain that just won't let off even for a moment.

Times ticking away and I get my official court date through. I have 4 weeks and then it's all or nothing. I told them I had no interest in taking their offer, so it really was going to be all or nothing!

About a week later I get a call from a width held number – the police will always call you on a width held number - I answer and yeah, the guy on the phone is another police officer. He checks who I am and asks me to come into the station as soon as possible for a chat. I state that I'm a few weeks out from my court date and that if they want any type of communication with me, then I want my solicitor present – I was pretty sure they were digging for any last bit of information they could use in court – but he assured me it was just to go over a couple minor things and that I would be fine coming in on my own. Begrudgingly I agreed and said I would come in first thing tomorrow afternoon. If they were going to fuck me, then I was damn sure going to be well rested.

I turn up at the station and hang around outside for a bit smoking 3 royals in about ten minutes and then go inside to face whatever the fuck is about to be thrown at.

I go through the usual rigger of who I am, who I'm here to see, blah, blah, blah... I get lead through to an interview room and there's a PCSO and an officer I have not seen before sat down. I take a seat and on the table in front of me is a tape recorder and an old style TV with a DVD player linked up to it.

We go through the footage again and I say exactly what I have said the whole time I've been asked. He counts how many times I hit the guy in the side and why I did it, I remember when it totalled about seven shots.

For some reason the officer then turns off the tape recorder and instructs the PCSO to leave the room. This is different to what I'm used to, so I'm now a little on edge. The officer leans in towards me and says "how many times did you hit him? Enough for him to learn his lesson!" I sit there a little unsure of what's just happened and the officer assures me that the case will be dropped and I won't need to go to court.

ADDICTED TO THE LIFE

He tells me that the other charge sergeant who has been dealing with my case is away on holiday for a few weeks and that he has taken over. I ask if he's sure and he states that he is. He says in two weeks to call him and the charges will all have been dropped. I'm not really sure what's going on, but I get up and walk out.

I wait the two weeks and then give him a call. True to his word, they are not going any further with the issue. He tells me that when he went through the whole of the footage from the night in question he believed there were reasonable grounds for my actions, and that if the guy pursued it any further then he would look at filing multiple assault charges for all the people that he assaulted during that incident.

I was in a state of shock.

Later upon hearing the news I found out that the guys mum had gone to the station to find out why the case of her poor, innocent son being savagely beaten by a gang of doormen had been dropped. She was informed of everything her son had done that night and that there was the possibility now of him being charged if it went any further.

As it turns out it would appear mummies little soldier hadn't mentioned that he had assaulted several people in the lead up to the incident with me. I guess that slipped his mind.

Seb 1 – drunken idiot 0.

ADDICTED TO THE LIFE

View from the Penthouse

Klute had very kindly terminated my employment. I was still working my day job, so money wasn't really an issue. I had enough to pay bills, rent and generally have a fairly care free existence.

As my weekends were free I had some spare time to enjoy myself. To be honest it was fairly boring, other than going out with Charlotte when she was free, I generally didn't have a lot of people to do things with. After a certain point working the doors tends to shift your social circle. You don't keep hours like regular people, so you mostly spend your time with other doormen. This means that when you have a weekend off, most of the people you have to hang out with are doormen and are working.

Having an abundance of free time was not good for me. People will tell you now that they always hear I'm doing something or another, this is because if I don't fill my time with things to do, then I'll fill my nose with stuff I shouldn't and get into trouble. I either function at 100 miles per hour or I am a shifty, irritable, bored, pain in the ass.

The nice thing about having a day job and weekends free was that Charlotte and I were able to do some actual couple stuff. We got to see each other at work which was fun. We snuck around chatting and seeing each other when no one was looking and people saw us together at didn't think anything of it – why would a pretty young girl like her be interested or have anything in common with me. On the evenings she worked late I would do the close down at the staff exit and grab a quick kiss good night whilst no one could see, it was quite sweet looking back on it. We even managed a day out to the zoo. I formed quite an attachment to a penguin that I named Pete.

I had done a bit of side work for some less savoury people here and there to keep myself amused and get a bit of extra pocket money. I was going to collect some money off a friend of mine from a club over in Poole – a little booster from another particular easy piece scam – that just so happened to be a strip club and night club combination. I had never been there before and I had never actually heard of the place either.

When I pulled up it was located down an alleyway between a multi storey car park and the main high street running through the town centre. It was on first impressions a dimly lit shit hole! Upon further inspection it was definitely a dimly lit shit hole!

I parked my car – keeping it within sight – and walked up to the entrance. I just remember it being empty. There was no one around, no queue, no customers and just Nick aka Mossy and Huggy Bear (Ashton) both looking bored and lent up against the wall.

I sort of knew them both, but just from the door circuit. Huggy was an up and coming junior bodybuilder and was built like a fucking tank! Nick and I had met at an engagement party a couple years before. We had chatted for about fifteen seconds in polite conversation, but nothing else had been said. He didn't remember our previous meeting, probably because

ADDICTED TO THE LIFE

it lasted fifteen seconds (for those of you that know Nick insert your own joke about his sex life) and he hadn't been that interesting and I thought he was a bit of a knob at our initial meet.

I asked if Bowler was about and they said he started in about twenty minutes, so he would probably be there in an hour. Bowler was for the most part an awful time keeper and one of the slowest moving people on this planet.

I lit a cigarette and hung around chatting shit with them awaiting Bowlers impending arrival. They told me about the club and took me for a look inside as I had never been inside before. I can honestly say it was not like any strip club I had ever been in (and not for a good reason.) There were about four girls inside, all sat at a table, all on their phones and not one single customer. The bar staff was just slumped against the bar desperately wanting anything to do and the Dj (Denbeigh) looked as equally unimpressed as everyone else in there.

I stood outside for a while and this figure came wondering down the alley way from next to my car. It turned out to be Neil the guy who owned the club. He said hello to the boys and then to me. He asked what I was doing and I told him I was waiting for Bowler to grab some cash. He asked who I was and I told him. I recognised him from other night clubs in town. To my surprise he knew exactly who I was and had heard all about me – normally that is never a good thing and doesn't really lead to anything positive – and asked why I was not working that night.

I went through the whole saga at Klute and told him about my upcoming legal issues. Neil asked if I had anything set up in the way of door work. I told him no, as it was a little tricky at the moment. People were not breaking down my door to offer work to a doorman who was looking at a custodial sentence for violence – it didn't quite give off the friendly and welcoming vibe they wanted.

Oddly Neil immediately offered me a job inside the strip club. I was a little surprised and reminded him that there was a chance in six weeks I would need a fairly substantial amount of time off – possibly two and a half years. He was adamant I should work for him. In his words, the place was full of cunts, always misbehaving and thought they were bad boys. He was quite happy to have a doorman that would not think twice about giving someone a thump and dragging them out. I could have the job as long as I wanted it. Seemed like a fair enough deal and nobody else was offering me anything, most clubs in Bournemouth would not touch me, so maybe going a couple of miles out the way would be a good idea.

I had gone out to pick up some cash and ended up with a job in a strip club. Obviously Charlotte was thrilled at the news of me now working at a strip club!

First night rolls around and it's time to see exactly what kind of animal I'm dealing with. I had a quick tour round again and got shown where the cameras were and where they were not. Nick and Huggy told me the people who came in were mainly scum and would only respond to violence. I went into the strip club and sat at my desk. I looked over at the

ADDICTED TO THE LIFE

girls and a couple of them looked up and gave me the once over – Teddy the usual guy had been moved upstairs to the Penthouse bar. Apparently the girls had become concerned that he wasn't being hands on enough when issues were kicking off with punters. I guess they were wondering if I was going to be any different.

Nothing was happening so I went out the front to join Nick. Huggy was not in that night. A couple of the other guys had turned up and were milling about the front entrance. A couple of guys came up to the door and went on through to the strip club. I was chatting and having a coffee, I figured there were about five or six girls and two customers, what could possibly happen? I got called back into the club by Jade (one of the dancers) who wanted me to remove the guys that had come in. Apparently one of them had been rude and then insulted her dead parents or something like that. I walked over to the table, the guy in question was sat with his back to me, but his mate saw me walking up. I told them that they had upset one of the girls and had to leave. The guys mate necked his drink and got up without any fuss.

For whatever reason, the guy in question decided he was going to make the rules as we went along. He got up and stated he would finish his drink as he walked out – not a problem for me. As we walked forward he told me not to touch him – not a problem for me as long as you're walking I don't fucking care. As we're walking out, Jade very kindly helps the situation by walking up and chucking a drink over the pair of us – you'll notice people, both girls and boys get really fucking brave when there's a doorman in between them and the person they're annoyed at. The guy obviously turns around to confront her and I spin him back in the direction of the door and tell him to keep walking. He turns and grabs hold of my belt and tells me he will knock me the fuck out. I tell him very calmly to just walk out. He lets go of my belt, but states again if I touch him he'll deck me. Okay mate just keep walking and we'll be fine. Once again he moves forward and we are pretty much at the dividing curtain to exit the strip club. For whatever reason – maybe because it's that I have come off as calm and not hit him that he seems to think he can try his luck with me – he turns and grabs my belt and again threatens me. Fuck it, now I'm in the mood for a bit of fun. I tell him to just leave, but as I'm doing so, I shift my stance to being a bit more side on and very quickly punch him in the throat. He stumbles back and I pounce on him – literally pounce on him, like a fucking leopard!

As he hits the deck I land swiftly on top of him. At this point I have completely lost my shit. I've got a finger in each of his eyes and nostrils and all pulling on his face shouting that I'm going to tear his fucking face off. As I'm pretty much mauling this kid, Bowler does the only sensible thing and instead of trying to get me off the guy, he draws the curtain so the girls in the strip club don't get disturbed. After a minute or so of me giving this kid a thorough going over Nick leans in and says it might be time to let the guy go. I let go and stand back, Bowler and Ben (the other doorman) help the guy up and he stumbles out the front door and off down the alley way. He has blood coming from his nose; ear, mouth and the corner of his eyes are already swollen and near enough shut. The manager Karston is lent against the wall outside having a fag and calls me over. I walk over and he offers me a fag. I have a smoke with him and then he tells me to go inside and clean myself up.

ADDICTED TO THE LIFE

Once I'm back inside I go to the bathroom, clean up and sit back on my stool at my desk and finish the coffee I made earlier – its cold. After about ten minutes Nick comes in and tells me that the girls had a chat with Karston and they want me in the club permanently.

I would start out with Nick and whoever else was on the front door with him that evening at 10pm when the club opened. There would be no customers until around 01:30/02:00am when the other bars would shut. So for four hours a night the rest of the staff and me had absolutely fuck all to do. I would split my time between talking to the guys on the front door, and having brief conversations with a couple of the girls who were a bit more sociable towards the door team. Mandy aka Angel was the club mum. That meant she was in charge of the girls and booked people to work each weekend. Mandy looked like most of the girls came down from Southampton. She was 5ft nothing, but wore massive stripper heels. She also had a phenomenally impressive, surgically enhanced rack. We became quite close as we worked there, not in a romantic sense, but just as really close friends. As she would know how many girls were due each week, I would text her and get a rough idea of what to expect from each passing weekend.

For reasons that are obvious, Charlotte wasn't overly thrilled about me continually messaging a stripper. I explained it was just work and that we were like a team when it came to looking after the strip club. I don't blame her for being a little sensitive about it; it wasn't the most fun thing for her. But as I said nothing romantic ever did or ever has happened with Mandy and I. To this day people do ask why we aren't together and it's simply that some people just make really good friends and that's it.

Things between Charlotte and I had picked up. We had been dating for a couple of months and still managed to keep things quiet. I had talked to Lloyd and Sam at work and they knew about us and our boss Eddie had come into the office and heard the conversation. Fast forward literally ten minutes and Charlotte was working on menswear and up comes Eddie with the store manager Karen and ask her if it's true that we're dating? Charlottes says yes and wouldn't you know it within a few hours everybody knew.

In the end it did make things easier as I didn't have to sneak around the store to see her and we got to go out on Valentine's Day like a proper couple without worrying about what people would say. She handled people brilliantly. The girls at work would ask her what she possibly saw in me, she said she got to see a different side to me than everybody else and that I was actually very sweet to be around. The boys just said they thought I was a legend as Charlotte was apparently far more attractive than I should have got – cheers for the confidence boost guys.

If there was anyone in the club who was being a little too keen with Mandy, then she would tell them she was married. And when they asked what does your husband think of you doing this? She would point at me and tell them to go ask him. If any girls would hit on me, then I would direct them towards the angry looking brunette in the corner and tell them she's my wife. If you told girls in there you had a girlfriend, then they would just say 'oh but she won't know.' Having a very angry looking bird, clutching a 6 inch stiletto in her hand helped

ADDICTED TO THE LIFE

drive the point across. It was a helpful set up as we both had partners and we helped keep the drunks away from each other.

People always thought that we talked too much at the club and that clearly something should have been going on. It wasn't the case. Because we both had partners and everyone else was pretty much single, it meant we were generally the only people each other could talk to about how working at a strip club affected our partners and we could have a chat that didn't end up in drunken sexual remarks and advances.

Now I say that the Kitty Club was a strip club and that is true, but that just does not paint you an accurate picture of what it was really like to be there. If you want to become a stripper or dancer or whatever is PC nowadays to say, then you would somewhere like FYEO (for your eyes only) or Spearmint Rhino, then you would call in and you would be brought in for an audition. That is standard procedure for most titty bars.

At the Kitty things worked a little differently. If you wanted to be a dancer, well then all you had to do was find someone who you knew worked there and ask them to get you a start or just ask one of the girls who was there and they would help you out. Now what this meant was we had the most eclectic range of strippers you could possibly imagine. Some of the girls we had come in were absolute knockouts, but sadly most of the girls that slithered through our doors were not the ripest of peaches off the tree!

The club had a small stable of regular girls who were there week in and week out and they were joined by whatever fillers happened to be in that week. The main problem was that to the girls this was a business. This was their living and the thought of another arguably more attractive girl coming in and being their competition was not something they wanted. If you had a girl come up to the club and start doing better, then fuck me did you get complaints from the other girls. All kinds of accusations were made about what she was letting the guys do in the private booths, but if we called every girl on every single infraction of the rules that were set out in there, then we would of had no fucking dancers at all! It was the Kitty club and the claws were definitely out.

Now working in a strip club you would get the same questions thrown at you night in and night out. The guys would say it must be amazing working in a strip club with all these birds around you. And the girls would ask if you thought they could be a stripper.

Now lads, just take a minute here to have a little think. Stop fluttering and getting a semi going over the thought of scantily clad girls in thongs, with their freshly spray tanned cheeks on display and their boobs just about being held in and up by the world's most resilient bit of neon coloured dental floss and really think.

If you have ever been in a relationship with a woman, then you will know that at times they can be a little temperamental. Most of the time they run and maintain like a fresh off the lot Ferrari, but sometimes when things get at them and I mean little things, especially to do with the destruction or misuse of their Mac make up, then they can have the tendency to go off the fucking boil. You try dealing with a group of women all making their living by

ADDICTED TO THE LIFE

looking more desirable than the other girls in there and at the same time having to share a very close proximity to them. All the while fighting to get ready and get out down amongst the hoards of drunken and naive men that are just itching to give their money to the first woman who makes them feel desired. It is not a good fucking time when they are all kicking off about each other. And who do they aim their displeasure at, well I'll give you a clue, it isn't the other girls, because they've got to appear friendly throughout the night in case one of the girls gets a client who wants two girls at once or a stag group comes in and wants the stag special.

It certainly isn't aimed at the manager who can fire them or the bar staff who recommend certain girls to customers. No it's the mug in the high VIS who serves no financial benefit to you what so ever. So lads it is not as much fun as you fucking think it is.

Ladies, I say this with all due respect. Yes anyone could be a stripper, you, yes you right now you could be a stripper, but on the same note if I didn't do more bugle than a brass band and fail my A-levels, and waste most of my time in my younger years stealing, dealing, defrauding and generally being a fucking nightmare, well I could be a doctor. You get what I'm trying to say? If you start your conversation with me by saying "I know I'm fat and I've got stretch marks and I'm not very attractive, but do you think I could be a dancer?" What do you think I'm going to say?........ Well love you're in the right place to fucking try!

The main thing that differentiated working at Penthouse from anywhere else I had worked was the fact everyone knew it was a shit hole. Everyone knew what kind of things to expect and the people that came with it. I was told from the off to watch out for the gypsies.

Now let me take a moment to clarify a few things, there is a whole lot of difference between a proper traveller or gypsy and some wannabe pikey. Proper travellers have the utmost respect in near enough every case I've dealt with them. A pikey will give it the lingo and just act like a fucking dick, and they're the ones that get reported about in the news and papers and what not as travellers and gypsies.

At my time at Penthouse I was fortunate enough to be introduced to a guy named Rossco. Rossco was essentially our main point of contact for the travellers in the area. If you had any type of problem or needed something sorted with them, then he was your go to guy. He would have a word and try and get the situation swiftly resolved. He reminded any of the guys that came in with him to be respectful towards us and in return we were respectful to them. To this day he is one of the few people I met as a customer in one of the clubs I worked that I am still good friends with. We recently had a night out to celebrate his 31st birthday – remember to not take pills off of strange black men in nightclubs, Rossco.

At this time I had taken up Jordan on his offer to train under him in MMA and I trained with him about four or five times a week. A long with this I decided that being with Charlotte was going well, but as long as I kept taking drugs then it wasn't going to advance to a better place. So I decided to get clean. I quit everything and I mean everything. I stopped cocaine, steroids, uppers, downers, pain killers, sleeping pills, alcohol and smoking.

COCAINE COMBAT

ADDICTED TO THE LIFE

It was not the smooth ride I had thought it was going to be. I had been using to varying degrees for around 14 years and that is a long time! My body handled the withdrawal without any real trouble, but my god the mental grasp it had was phenomenal. I didn't know what was happening, I had gone from feeling nothing for so long to suddenly feeling everything and it felt like the volume in my life had been turned up 1000% and it scared the shit out of me.

It didn't make things easier or better for Charlotte and I like I thought it would. I would have days where I felt depressed and anxious and days where I felt really good, my mood swings would go up and down like a yoyo. My sex drive was up and down as well and it was an absolute nightmare at times. If I had told Charlotte what was going on with me then she probably would have understood and been supportive, she had supported every other idea I had, but I couldn't talk to her about it. I wasn't from a family where we shared things and I wasn't from friendship circles where you had been encouraged share how you felt, it was a sign of weakness, that I would be less of a man if I did, so I just slowly drove myself insane. The only thing deep down I really needed was for someone to give me a hug and tell me I'm alright, but showing anyone that I needed them in anyway was against everything I had come to know.

We broke up a couple of times for a week and both times I apologised and promised I would try better. I did admit to her once that I was just a bit scared by things, I didn't go into specifics, I'd lost my bottle at that point and just kept apologising and she forgave me and off we went again.

To show how my life went when I was unsupervised and left to my own devices I'll tell you this story as a prime example of what happened during one of the times we were on a pause.

So I went out on a night off with a friend of mine, a female friend – nothing sinister just a drinking companion – and we met up with a couple of other people we both knew from the clubbing scene. So we end up in a bar, I don't remember which one and her friend wants to go pick up – my role as bag man had ended in the run up to seeing Charlotte - so they go off to meet a guy and pick up. After about 20 minutes I've not heard anything and I give her a call. She tells me the guys they went to meet have got them at this house and they can't get away. So I tell her to give me the address and I'll drive over. I head down and meet them at the corner of this street near my childhood house and this Mercedes pulls up. It's one of the guys and he wants to see who this guy is the girls have called, so I hope out the motor and low and behold we know each other really well – from a number of different business ventures – and he invites me to the house. So I end up in this house, well I say a house, it's a brothel. A quiet night out for a few drinks ends up with me sat down with one of the heads of the local drug syndicate, shovelling in cocaine from this Tupperware box, hookers wandering about and this girl who had called me to rescue her sitting in the corner looking very uneasy.

Shortly into my time at Penthouse Huggy got himself a new day job and had to give up his weekends with us. So how do you replace this giant, oversized piece of mahogany man

ADDICTED TO THE LIFE

candy? You call your gigantic, slightly more stable than you bromance and ask him to help out for a bit.

The best thing about Karston as our boss was that he understood how things worked. He gave us leeway that wouldn't get with many other managers. He knew what type of people we were dealing with and he knew how to handle the girls. Being a doorman himself he knew the grey area that you worked within. Allow me to explain, now say you're removing a guy from a club and your manager is watching and this guy you're wrestling with is struggling like a bitch. You are well within your right as a doorman to use justifiable force to help get him or her under control. So you do the smart thing and give the guy a swift body blow to deflate his desire to fight and struggle with you. Now you are as I said perfectly within your right to do that. However, all the manager sees is you taking a pot shot at a customer out of context and because your manager has had to sit an SIA licensed course, he or she thinks she is now a confirmed expert in the world of door work and being such, he or she now has you bollocked and fired. All that for simply for doing your job under the guide lines set by the SIA, oh the irony.

There were an unprecedented number of fights, altercations, violent incidents and confrontations at the Penthouse in comparison to anywhere else I have ever worked and probably will ever work. It was a den of cunts, where only cunts came and only cunts seemed to be allowed. It would take over a hundred thousand words alone to just list most of things that went on at this place. In fact I may have to bring out another book after this one about Penthouse all on its own.

Our job was not made any easier by our boss Neil. We would have regulars – these were the cunts that came here every week, because no one else would have them – that would continually cause trouble. They would do something, fight someone or deal something or insult one of the girls and try to start a fight with us and we would tell them to fuck off and that they're banned and they would then go up to Neil and talk all nice to him, low and behold they would be allowed back in the club. There is absolutely no point in having doormen if you don't let them do their job. So now we end up with a club full of people who know they can cause trouble and there will be absolutely no repercussion. So essentially you've got a den of cunts with a feeling of superiority over the staff.

I'm outside with Nick and Scott and a couple of the other guys, it's around eleven, so there is fuck all going on inside the club. I'm chain smoking royals as was my way of coping without the loss of cocaine and vodka in my life. This murky figure starts to emerge from the shadows of the alley way. Now no one, but us (the guys who work at the club) come out from those shadowy corners, so my natural instinct is its some degenerate or one of the boys. As the figure becomes clearer, it's apparent that the figure is female (only fucking just) and it slowly comes closer and closer to us. On first inspection I assume this is most definitely a hooker! The pale, pasty skin, god awful self made looking prison tattoos and general guise of the beast make it's hooker like nature apparent. This thing can be likened to the creature emerging from the black lagoon comes past the front door, it slows and turns its head, bobbing up as if to see some sign of humanity in the area. It turns towards us at the entrance

COCAINE COMBAT

ADDICTED TO THE LIFE

of the club; I and all the boys quickly try to shift our focus from creature, fearing it has the same mythical powers of medusa and will turns us all to stone with just one look. As we do it mutters the most chilling words ever known to a doorman "is this the kitty club entrance? I'm due to start work here, is Angel about?" Well fuck me.....

The things that dance, well I say dance, I mean have some sort of a seizure on stage and try to pass it off as dancing were a sight in themselves. We had one girl who came to work at the club for about three weeks and then swiftly disappeared back into the depravity from which she came. This particular girl whose name I forget was busted one Saturday night at the Penthouse for doing coke. The next weekend she appears in thong and 6 inch heels as a new dancer. Our screening process was very thorough! The problem was this creature, like most girls who come into the club and saw the girls dance, naturally assumed that they could just as easily dance. Now this is in itself true, any girl can once they've turned 18 become a stripper, but it is a very big difference in earning ability between a girl who can dance and a girl who can't. Never underestimate the ability and physical strength of a good stripper; it is not as easy as it looks!

This girl got on stage and just put one hand round the pole and then......... Just shook her body from side to side. Dance routine complete. It was one of the most entertaining and horrendous car wrecks of a routine I have ever witnessed! Bye bye love.

My night was broken into three sections. Firstly my arrival at around 10pm to open the club and more importantly find someone to make the coffee, secondly at 11pm I would go for a five minute break to evacuate my bowls and then thirdly at 1am when I would go to evacuate my bowls for the second time – yes the club literally bored the shit out of me.

One particular time I was in the strip club and things are pretty quiet, we have a group of lads in and they're having a drink and a few dances. Suddenly this prick decides he should be on the main stage, I casually get up from my stool and get up on to the stage and nicely ask the guy to get down and leave the dancing to the girls – the guys are all spending money and if he can get down and behave, then they will keep spending money and the girls will stay happy and stop bitching about each other for a while longer – and rejoin his friends. He ignores me and carries on swinging, so I grab him and he refuses to let go of the pole and tells me he works for the town watch and can do what he likes. I take this on board for a second and then drag him to the floor and thump him in the face a couple of times. Whilst he's pinned down I calmly radio Scott to come in the strip club. Scott takes his time. Happily wandering into the club – as it's around 1am he naturally assumed he was covering my routine 5 minute break – and looks up to find me on top of some guy on stage. He comes over and grabs the guys' legs, whilst laughing that he thought I was having a break, because I sounded so nonchalant over the radio. We laugh; I lift the guy up and start carrying him towards the back exit of the kitty club. We get into the alley way and the guy is shouting how he's going to take our jobs and we'll never work again, blah, blah, blah. As it happens Scott has a pretty smart idea. He notices the dumpster lid is up, so he looks at me, looks at the dumpster and smiles. I know exactly what he's thinking and I smile back. One, two, three and into the dumpster the guy goes, I close the lid and back into the club we go.

ADDICTED TO THE LIFE

Now with the layout of the strip you can't see what's going on in the booths behind the stage, you have to walk around and physically check everything. As no one comes into the Penthouse bar upstairs until about 2am you have to deal with the strip club. When the radio goes off before 2am it's a safe bet that there is something going on in the strip club.

So I'm on the front door and the radio goes off, I look at Nick who's beside me, we know the upstairs bar is empty, so must be the strip club. I run in through the curtains and nothing is happening, must be the booths behind the stage. I run around to them and straight down in to the VIP booth, but as I do I catch my foot on something and nearly stumble straight through the curtain. I take a quick scan inside and everything seems to be fine, I mouth to the girl are you okay and she nods back yes. I'm a little confused, but everything seems good, so I turn around to make my way back through and out of the club. I notice that on the floor, in the galley way booth, there is some hair sticking out from behind the curtain on the floor into the walk way. This is odd. I take a moment to let it sink in and then move towards the curtain, I open it and the guy on the sofa throws both his hands up and starts saying I never touched her, I never touched her, and she just stopped moving. Well I'm no Sherlock Holmes, but it dawns on me that as I was running in, the stripper is doing some sort of exotic floor dance and being that she was about 6ft2 and out of heels, she must have leant back as I was running past and low and behold I have kicked her square in the fucking head. I did the only thing I could think of and told the guy to keep his hands to his fucking self, gave the girl a nudge and walked back to the front door and told Nick it was a false alarm.

Now over a bit of time at the club things got a bit heated between a couple of the girls. There was a bit of a standoff between Angel and Jade for the role of head bitch in charge. Jade was slagging Angel off and Angel was less than amused about this. One night the girls are absolutely fucking shit faced. Neil has come round and as its early and no one is coming; he's decided to give the girls a couple of bottles of wine to keep them in the party mood. Over the course of a few hours people start coming in and the girls are fucking shitfaced! One poor guy is lent up against the bar with Jade and one of the other girls talking to him. Whilst the guy is distracted by the other girl, Jade is reaching in his jacket pocket and pulling out notes of cash. Now I know shit goes on in strip clubs and every other fucking club and I know door staff normally get the rep of being cunts and letting shit going on and protecting the girls when they do this type of thing, but we are not going to stand by and watch someone getting robbed in front of are fucking eyes, that's bullshit!

At the end of the night the boys and I have a word with Karston and tell him what's happened and that we won't be ignoring that type of shit here. Either she goes or we go, because we're not getting the blame for that type of shit and we're not going to sit by and let it happen.

We come in the next week to find Jade is no longer dancing at the club. Karston has told Neil about and Neil has dealt with it. Yeah all well and good, until Neil has made her the clubs promotions manager – I'm fucking serious, that was the move he made. You take the girl whose just been fired for robbing customers and put her in charge of generating more custom.

COCAINE COMBAT

ADDICTED TO THE LIFE

Fortunately the role of promotions manager lasted less than a month and Jade was fired. Who would have thought putting a mouthy, robbing stripper in a suit would not instantly transform her into a business guru?!

Around the same time as the whole Jade and Angel power struggle, Scott had had enough and let his license expire. This meant I needed a replacement, but where the fuck do you find another man mountain? It's not like these freaks of nature grow on trees. Luckily I had another friend called Big Dave. Who as it happens was probably the only person who was bigger than Scott. I called Dave and said I had guaranteed weekend work for him if he wanted it. I told him all about the club and he decided he would come down and give it a shot.

Dave was perfect. I put him in the strip club and worked the front door with Nick. Dave didn't have any interest in people, making friends, the girls or even talking to people. He was a physically huge deterrent with the power of ten men. Exactly what the club needed.

One of my personal favourite moments and it summed up Dave's personality in perfect form. Maddison was one of our regular girls at the club and one night she happened to decided for whatever reason she would try to get to know Dave a little better.

Maddison walks up to Dave as he's leant against the wall watching the usual goings on of the club and begins chatting to Dave.

Maddison: Dave, do you like food?

Dave: Uh, yes.

Maddison: Do you like carvery dinners?

Dave: Uh, yes.

Maddison: Can I buy you a carvery dinner?

Dave: Yeah.....wait...will you be there too?

Maddison: Yeah!

Dave: Oh in that case no.

This ended any attempt by any girl at the club attempting to get to know Dave better.

Around this time Karston had decided to leave the club and get a more relaxing day job, just like a normal person. I was still working at the department store and had pretty much had enough of Penthouse, so I decided to make a move to a different venture.

ADDICTED TO THE LIFE

All About The Mooney

I had spoken a bit to a friend of mine, the aforementioned Jordan Mooney who happened to own several businesses, one of which happened to be a security company – Vanguard as I mentioned earlier. I met Jordan pretty much by weird coincidence. He happened to have bought my old childhood home and had some old post from my family there (we had moved out several years prior, so fuck knows what was still being sent there) and his tattoo parlour was where I was having some more work done at the time.

The one thing I liked about Jordan more than anything else was that he wasn't full of shit. You meet so many people in the various nooks of the night club industry that are just bullshitting their way through life, trying to bring some fake meaning or sense of achievement in their pathetic, unfulfilled lives. It's the typical pantomime charade – parents have money, you get a nice house to pose in for pictures on Instagram, they get a hire car thanks to mum and dad, it's usually a range rover and then all the girls think OMG he's so cool. Jordan was always on hand for his guys, if you got into trouble at work, he was only a phone call away. He also helped me with business ideas and general advice with a lot of things.

Charlotte and I had gone on holiday to Barcelona for her 18th birthday and the holiday hadn't ended as well as we would have hoped. We had been together for about 7 months at this point and she wanted to hear the L word from me. She had hinted about it on holiday and I hadn't done or said anything about it.

We got back to Bournemouth and after a week of awkward tension she said she loved me and I said I didn't love her. In all honesty I did love her, I was just fucking terrified, I still couldn't understand why someone like her loved me, she had hinted about it after a couple of months of us being together and I just had flashbacks all the time to growing up. Everyone who I ever cared about had at some point either abandoned me or really hurt me at some point. There had been times for months where I hadn't spoken to my mum after we would fall out, my dad and I had an extremely strained relationship and in my mind if I said I love you out loud and she left then I really didn't know what I would do with myself, I just wasn't mentally or emotionally stable enough to cope with things. I did however accept I needed help and went into a treatment programme to help me find a way to cope.

Jordan had a lot of clubs and bars available, so it was a question of shuffling me around and seeing where I would fit in. Conveniently he had the contract for a strip club in town Spearmint Rhino. They wanted guys who had experience in working at similar venues and Jordan sent me over there to cover some shifts.

Now after spending a year at the Kitty Club you would think I would have had enough of tits and ass, but this was how a strip club was meant to be. It was a nice change to what I had got used to.

ADDICTED TO THE LIFE

The club was set up over 3 floors, you had the entrance, reception and toilets on the ground floor, the second floor was the main, and bar and then up the stairs to the top floor for private dances. The club averaged about 20-30 girls dancing each weekend and unlike the Kitty Club these girls were actually vetted and auditioned before they were given shifts – thus insuring you had girls people actually wanted to pay money to see naked!

One of the funny things is how irrelevant nudity becomes to you as a bouncer. I'm stood against the wall, dead centre in front of the stage and there is a girl topless, jiggling, stretching, and bending and gyrating in front of me and all I'm thinking is what time is we doing the roosters run for a chicken wrap? It was almost nice for me to catch up with a friend. I was watching the stage show and on comes the daughter of my former local pub landlord and landlady. The odd thing to most people was I didn't really bat an eye lid at seeing her come off the stage half naked, she walked up and we both said hello and started asking how each other's families were doing. Hayley was always very chatty to my dad when we used to drag him out for a few. And I caught up how her little ones were doing and how Steve her husband and another old friend of mine were. Odd to look back and think you've got half naked chics everywhere and drunken guys waving money around and we're stood in the middle of it all discussing school districts and old people hobbies.

The girls were very business orientated, there was no sitting around drinking or fucking about on your phone, they were there to earn and with so many of them they really went for it! They didn't waste time chatting to the door staff when there were guys in the club that had the possibility of spending money on them – well except Hayley, we always had a catch up chat on shift. Since we were friends I'd point guys in her direction whenever anyone asked me who was worth getting a dance off – and buying them drinks.

The job was pretty easy as far as it goes. You spend an hour in a pair down on the front door checking ids and keeping an eye on the girls who went for a smoke and then you did an hour up on the main stage keeping an eye on the customers and girls inside. I was normally paired up with Eddie. He was the same age as me, had a mutual love of Staffordshire bull terriers and chatted about MMA and women. The other guys on shift were usually Gary – who was probably the most ripped 40yr old on the fucking planet, Big Tomasz the largest heavyweight MMA fighter in the country at that time and Winnie who was the head doorman. I'll be honest other than being a successful businessman you couldn't really find out anything else about Winnie. His age was a well guarded secret. His son Kian was the DJ, but Winnie didn't look old enough to have a son of that age. I imagine if you ever wanted to find out his age you'd have to cut him open like an oak tree and count the rings.

My time spent there was pretty much completely drama free and I got to do some shifts with Scott on the odd occasion which was always a bonus.

As I mentioned Jordan had the security contract for a series of clubs and bars so I got moved around. One of the nicest venues I did some work at was over in Christchurch at an

ADDICTED TO THE LIFE

upscale bar called Soho. Soho was an over 25 bar and being so tended to attract a more upmarket and professional crowd.

Unfortunately not all the venues Jordan had were as nice. Scott and I got sent over to a place called the Rydal. The Rydal was a fucking sess pool and attracted a distinctly lower class of cunt than we had ever seen at the Penthouse. The pair of us was sent for one specific reason and that was to sort out the never ending sea of trouble that was continually going on every fucking weekend. It was hinted that as the pub was so far off the beaten track - and that you were pretty much the only back up each other was going to get – that it would be a good idea to take a little something extra with us to level the playing field.

Scott and I turned up at the dreary looking, skank filled pit that was the Rydal with duster each secreted about per persons. Upon arriving we found out that a number of fights with various teams of door staff had taken place and the locals had pretty much been given the run of the place. The bar manger was of no fucking help as they didn't enforce any rules and when you were telling people they had to leave, they would tell them it was okay to stay. After one shift having dealt with nothing but trouble and removed various groups of degenerates only for the management to allow them to come right back in, it was decided that some places just can't be fixed. We never stepped foot in that shit hole again and I can honestly say I never fucking will.

I did get to team up with Scott again at a venue just down the round from Soho called Dukes. This was where the people that weren't nice enough to come into Soho went for a drink. In my brief time there was nothing really noteworthy which took place. The usual removal of boys and girls who couldn't handle their drinks. A long with the occasional wannabe Rocky Balboa being sent packing, but otherwise a pretty smooth run.

During my time working for Jordan I hit a slight financial snag. My day job as a securities manager had come to an end after I had finally had enough of putting up with my moronic store manager. In a meeting where he was criticising the work me and my guys had been doing for him I finally had enough and told him I'd had enough of the job and enough of him. Not the smartest move when you have bills and rent to pay, but everyone reaches a breaking point and after 9 months of smiling and putting up with his bullshit I hit mine.

I did a bit of work for an agency and ended up in the exciting world of banking. This lasted 6 weeks. I am not built for office work and 8 hours a day typing.

Luckily a new bar was opening up and they were looking for door staff for contracts between 2 and 6 nights per week.

COCAINE COMBAT

ADDICTED TO THE LIFE

Going Up Market

I had my first MMA fight under Jordan Miller and had won by guillotine in under 25 seconds – if he can take drug abusing, unfocused, mentally questionable lunatic like me then he can teach anyone – and my counselling sessions had helped me to open up a bit more and get more of a grasp of how to focus, handle and more importantly cope with things.

One thing had become very clear it my brief period of enlightenment and that was that I really had fucked up with Charlotte. When your therapist makes you aware that you got rid of the only person who unconditionally loved you, you do get the sudden realisation that you made a mistake. "Yeah Harry, no one else will put up with your shit." Inside joke.

It was grovelling time! I was still working at Spearmint Rhino on weekends, but I had left my job at the department store and was working for a bank in town. I was sat on my bed staring at my phone for about 2 hours when I got the balls to call Charlotte and put it all on the line. After what was a very in depth conversation she agreed to meet me. A couple of days later I picked her up from her aunt's house and we went for a walk in the countryside, I found a spot where I used to walk my dogs, told I was sorry for everything and that I loved her. After a very lengthy conversation that involved me apologising and explaining what I had learnt whilst in counselling, she relented and agreed to start seeing me again and I would have to prove myself before she began to trust me again. She made it clear if this happened again then that was definitely the end of us and any further chances.

It had been few weeks and I was awaiting the start date the new club and Charlotte and I were getting on better. She even got involved in helping organise Jordan's MMA night that I was fighting on next. I won the fight by guillotine in under 20 seconds and celebrated with a pizza and a quiet night in with her. Unfortunately my next fight didn't go so well and I not only lost, but I damaged my septum and partially tore my hernia that had been surgically repaired a few years previously. I can't put it down to anything going wrong with my training under Jordan; it was down to me getting back into my aesthetics rather than my training. I had started using steroids again and my cardio and training had suffered which left me pretty much an ineffective mess when it came to the fight.

I started my job full time at the new club just before Christmas and the venue was very up market, it had a strict dress code and was all about cocktails and high end prices. They were going for the high end crowd and trying to deter the hoards of dishevelled drunks that descended on Bournemouth looking for WKD buckets and 2 for 1 shot.

My time at this place lasted for a few months. The venue was nice, but it just wasn't for me. I had moved into a flat with Jordan which was fun, but working almost every night doesn't leave that much free time when it comes to a relationship and quality time.

The only mildly memorable thing that did happen was on New Year's Eve when Charlotte unfortunately peaked a little too soon and my dad had come pick her up and drop

ADDICTED TO THE LIFE

her back to mine. I came home around 4am and she was sat up waiting for me to apologise. It was slightly odd being on that side of the apology, but it was funny and we laughed about it.

I did get a call about an incident that was happening across town at Klute. My mate Matt was on the door and some fucking retard came up and pulled a gun on him and disco Dave. When I say retard, this is the guy that was apparently the enforcer for the muppet that had wanted to fight me at V and ghosted into the night without so much of a word. Matt responded in typical manner and laughed at the guy – there really is not much to do in that situation. If someone is close enough to blow your brains out, then there isn't much you can do, so just accept what will be will be and try and think of a cool line to go out on – and it turned out the gun was a fake. The guy just turned and ran off when his macho move had got no response.

I took a job at a freight company out in Verwood; literally a couple of minutes from Charlotte's family home in attempt to have a bit more of a normal life. It was also around this time that I looked at going to university. I had gone back to college and gotten my diploma in performing arts, but I hadn't used it for anything and as I was just seemingly going from job to job without any really future or stability and I thought applying wouldn't hurt. Charlotte was great and encouraged me; she thought I had been wasting my potential for far too long and that I would do well if and when I got to university.

My job at the freight company probably lasted for about 6 months. The hours were long and the commute was about an hour each way. I was constantly tired and I had stupidly given up on counselling a few months back as everything with me seemed to be working out, I figured I didn't need it any more.

Sadly this is the point where any of you rooting for me to keep momentum and thinking at least he's got his personal life under control are going to be very disappointed.

I was not the great boyfriend that I thought I was. I was there, but I wasn't really there. I didn't make much of an effort to show Charlotte how I felt or that I cared. I would do really big gestures on Valentines and special occasions, but the rest of the time I just wasn't great. In my mind because I wasn't a drug user so then I was automatically a great person. That wasn't the case. I was a better person for it, but it didn't mean I was a good person by other peoples standards, at that time I was just a bit too blind to see it. One evening Charlotte sat down with me and said she didn't think it was working anymore. With the effort I was putting in when we pretty much lived together, it was never going to work when I moved to London for university – I got accepted on an actual degree and had decided to take the offer.

That was to be the end and the beginning of a very bleak chapter....

ADDICTED TO THE LIFE

Downward Spiral

I had moved out of Jordan's flat after we had a disagreement – the thing with me and Jordan is we are very much the same. When we think we are right, there is no way to change our minds. Great friends, but awful housemates... Quick thank you to his girlfriend at the time Alicia whom literally acted like mine and Scott's mum and looked after us like we were slightly retarded children – and had now moved into the spare room at Lloyd and Alex's house.

I remember finding the remains of a very small bag of cocaine in amongst the few worldly possessions I had, remember laying out this tiny line on the kitchen table and looking at it. I had not touched a fucking speck since I went clean at the start of mine and Charlotte's relationship. I looked at it and I fucking knew that if I did it, even that small amount then I would be back in a world of trouble. Back down the rabbit hole I fell.....

I took a job back at Klute with some of the boys from before as I thought it would help keep me busy and my mind off things. I had made an attempt to salvage things with Charlotte. I had asked to meet her and talk to see if there was anything we could do. Finding yourself in a box room with a bag of clothes and your dog – love you Freddy - will put things into perspective. We met at a cafe and I asked her how she was and we began chatting. The conversation did not go great. Now only a small handful people know about that meeting with her and what happened and I've kept it that way for a long fucking time, not even my family know what happened, but this is probably as good a time as any to share and may be you'll see the next few pages in a clearer light by knowing this.

During our conversation I told her that I didn't want to get back together and break up again, I thought that was a waste of time. She didn't quite know what I meant, so I showed her. I pulled out a ring and asked her to marry me....... I'll give you a minute to let that sink in....... And now back to the rest of the book.

My next few weeks were not good. I hit town every fucking night, I rolled into my day job after not sleeping and doing bumps of coke in the toilets during my breaks to keep me going. I would then go home and start my night off again. I had started doing so much coke that the only way to afford it was go back to my old job of pharmaceutical distribution again. After one particular night where I was still up partying my phone went off. It was a message from Charlotte saying she was worried about the amount of partying I was doing. I was being tagged in every club every night and she asked if I was using again. I told her it was and it was none of her business. I became quite a fucking arsehole if I'm being brutally honest. It was a defence mechanism. That night I carried on through to the next morning. My alarm went off, I was literally doing a massive line off the kitchen table and I looked at the phone, turned it to silent and decided I had enough of that job. I never answered a call or went back.

ADDICTED TO THE LIFE

I worked a couple of nights a week and the rest of the time I just got mangled. I would turn up to a shift on Saturday night having not slept for two days and just play it off like I had a cold. I think people just accepted it or they just didn't really care. As long as I could stand there and do my job, then they left me be.

Things became unsettled at Klute. John had sold his half of the business and a new guy had bought it and his idea was that the reason the club didn't do well and attracted the wrong type of people was because of the look of the door team. He brought in a new uniform policy – apparently people don't feel like fighting if the doorman is wearing a tie and waist coat – and brought in other door staff to show us how it should be done.

The guys they brought in made it very clear it was us versus them, they were without doubt the biggest bunch of fucking retards I had ever seen. If the club was quiet, the new head door would turn to Matt and tell him to get rid of one of his guys.

We all eventually left for other venues. The only real good thing that came out of my brief return to Klute was my friendship with Dom really grew. He had been the only person I had told about my issues and the things that had gone on with Charlotte and he really helped to try and keep me levelled out and support me, as it was clear I wasn't coping. I will always be grateful to him for that. To this day he is one of my closest friends and even more impressively I actual act like a normal connected human being around his son Mason. Which considering how little parental instincts and patience I have is a real show of our friendship.

Now me being the smart, clear headed and rational person I was at that time I thought the best place for me to back and work at was the Penthouse.

So on this particular shift one of Nicks' female friends appears at the club to work as a dancer. I'm in the Kitty club killing time by chatting with girls and generally fucking around, when Nick brings Vicky in and introduces her to us.

As there's not much to do during the opening four hours of the shift, Vicky and I spent the majority of the evening fucking around. When you work in strip clubs long enough you can pick up a couple of moves, these moves were something that Scott and I would occasionally showcase – if you've ever seen a 22st man worm and pole dance, then you know it's breath taking – for the amusement of the girls and every so often some very bewildered looking customers.

The night drew to a close without so much an incident which made a nice change. As I walk out the front door, the boys are stood around having a chat. Just so happens that Vicky is out there as well. Nick says he has to go upstairs and do the paperwork and chat with Karston. Vicky asks me how long will Nick be and without missing a step Scott chimes in saying oh he'll be a while – always on point as a wingman – Vicky then states that Nick is giving her a lift home, but she doesn't want to wait around too long. As a gentleman I offer my services, conveniently she lives a five minute drive from my house. She graciously accepts my offer and as we walk around to my car, I look up at the window of the club reception only to see Nick scowling down towards me. I flip him the bird and off we go.

ADDICTED TO THE LIFE

As happens in most clubs you get the odd dispute between couples. We were no different, well other than the fact most of the birds were meaner than their boyfriends. This particular time a guy and his girl were having a domestic that appeared to be escalating a bit. Suddenly this guy rears back and smashes his bird right in the mouth. All bets are off now, me, Scott and Nick leapt off the front door and immediately onto the guy. We manoeuvre him away and check on the girl, she's a bit shocked, but not as bad as she could be. Scott and I are shoving the dipshit down the alley and telling him never to come back again, whilst Nick is getting the girls friends to see if she wants to press charges or get medical attention. As we're walking back to the club door the guy pops up beside me and says something, on instinct I turn around a slap him right across the face. He drops to the floor like he's been shot and before he can get up; his girlfriend is on me like a fucking rash. He's just lumped the shit out of her and she's on me threatening to have me killed for giving her boyfriend a bit of a slap....You're fucking welcome to each other!

My time in Penthouse was much different this time around. I was actively using at work and without being in a committed relationship I was also throwing after parties.

The parties created some of the most memorable and unsanitary occasions I think anyone could ever imagine.

Now this is not only one of my favourite stories from my time on the doors, but one I will state is arguably the greatest door work story of all time!

As the Kitty club is on the ground floor and the Penthouse bar is upstairs with no lift. So if people with disabilities would come in, then we would allow them to spend the last hour drinking in the Kitty club when everyone else was moved upstairs for the last hour.

This night we have an old boy in a wheelchair that had been coming in fairly frequently staying in the Kitty club after it closed. We allowed his mates to stay with him and get drinks from the upstairs bar and bring them down to him, that way he didn't have to end his night just because he couldn't get up the stairs. Along with him and his group of friends on this particular we also had a young lad in a wheelchair with a separate party of mates, who we also allowed to stay downstairs and carry on partying for the last hour.

I'm on the front door with Nick, generally doing nothing, just keeping an eye on the drunks smoking outside and making sure that no one was pissing about. One of the girls from the Kitty comes out and asks me to go have a word with the groups in there as they're getting a bit rowdy. I go in and there's some sort of Barney going on between the guys in the wheelchairs – apparently over who has the better wheelchair. I go in and politely explain that we have been very gracious in letting them stay inside after closing the strip club and that if they take the piss they can fuck off out of the club. All smiles and nods of agreement and I'm back on the front door enjoying a late night coffee and sparking up a royal.

No longer than chipping out my fag and enjoying two mouthfuls of coffee do I get called back into the Kitty club to speak to the two groups again. I go in and the boys in wheelchairs appear to be having some type of modern day jousting match with each other - I

ADDICTED TO THE LIFE

suppose that's one way to settle a disagreement – whilst their mates are trying to calm the situation down. I call Big Dave in and he helps me clear the groups out the club and into the alley outside. Dave turns to me and asks if I want him to stay on the front door in case anything kicks off. I tell him that it's two guys in wheelchairs, what the fuck could happen? Oh how wrong could I have been?!

The two guys in the wheelchairs continue their argument. I walk over to intervene and try to get them both to leave. As I'm doing so, one of the guys who are friends with the younger guy comes up and does his best to help me. For whatever reason the older guy takes offence to this and grabs hold of the guys' shirt, pulls himself out of his wheelchair and starts punching the guy in the face. To his fucking credit the guy pushes the old boy off him and carries on trying to calm the situation down. For whatever one of the local boys Jack comes running over and starts having a go at the guy who has just been punched in the face and gets mouthy with him. The guy who has been helping me and remained calm the whole time has had enough and thumps Jack in the face, Jack hits the deck and pops back up like a really startled Jack in the box toy. The next thing you know everyone is running over to get involved and within a minute we have a full scale riot going on. There are bodies everywhere, clusters of people fighting who have had nothing to do with the incident. As I'm stood having my own stand up exchange with some random cunt, someone runs past and the old boy tries to grab him, but as he does the force of the guy running pulls him out of his wheelchair and he ends up laid on the floor with his arms stuck up in the air shouting "help me, help me please!" I'm busy punching away at someone and laughing my ass off at the same time. After about ten minutes five squad cars and two riot vans arrive to nullify the brawl. As everything calms down and the boys and me are heading back inside to shut the club Big Dave turns to me and says "just two guys in wheelchairs, what could go wrong?"

It wasn't all violence, drugs and chavs at the Penthouse, the boys and me also did a little bit here and there to help people out. One of our regulars who would come by for a coffee and chat was clamper Dave. Him and his Mrs Jo would stop in on his rounds and chat with us to pass the time; they were both very nice and would bring down biscuits and sweets occasionally for us. I remember Jo asked us if we would sponsor her daughter for some event at school, she said most of the kids in the class would get a few pounds from their parents – they were only young kids, so it's not like they had endless amounts of friends or money – however the boys and me didn't want to risk her looking embarrassed at the school, so we all chucked in a tenner each just to make sure she won. She did and we even offered to come down to her sports day and take part in the adult races for her as Dave might be a bit tired from working nights. See we were a giving lot.

This story I like to refer to as 'chicken strippers.' I had been running about all day drinking and dropping bits off to people and Lloyd had told me about a BBQ that some girls from FYEO were having. He was hooking up with one of the girls from there, so later on we headed down. As I said I had been running about all day and was fucking starving! I walked in and headed straight for the BBQ and devoured a series of chicken skewers. I offered them around, but Alex refused as he believed they looked a little undercooked. He was not wrong as it turned out.

COCAINE COMBAT

ADDICTED TO THE LIFE

A few hours into the party and I was not feeling fantastic. I went to find a toilet only to find the downstairs toilet didn't lock or have any toilet roll. I went back out to the BBQ and was trying to find the boys to say I was going to head off for a bit, but instead I bump into Alex who's talking to two very attractive young ladies and the comment "if you want weird sex stories talk to Seb." So here I am beginning to sweat profusely and trying not to shit myself whilst holding down some flirty banter with two very attractive ladies. I eventually made my way out and towards to my car, but low and behold the fight could not go on. I got two feet from my car and shit my pants. I had a quick change in the street by the car, flung my underwear into a neighbouring garden, cleaned myself off with a bottle of water and my dog blanket for walking Freddy and left the mound of shit curb side and headed home.

I awoke the next morning to find the boys had gone onto walkabout with the girls and my mate Adam had joined them. He was passed out on the sofa when I came downstairs. I started making breakfast and getting the info on what happened after I left. Adam told me he turned up shortly after I had gone and that when he pulled up, he got out of his car and stepped in a massive pile of shit. Turns out he had parked in my spot and the shit was mine and to top it off, he was wearing flip flops and as he got out the car it came off and he stepped bare foot into my shit.

Things had changed at the Penthouse – it was no longer the fun mixing pool it had been. Karston was replaced by Jessie. Jessie was a 20yr old with no managerial or nightclub experience. He was however good friends with one of Neil's close friends who, if you believe rumours was also an extremely dangerous coke dealer who had taken control of most of the drug scene in the area after his release from prison for drugs and weapons charges. Now I can't confirm or deny any of the things I heard, because I never once caught the guy in question with or saw him doing coke. So to me he was just a regular guy who came by the club to see Jessie and spend money on the girls. He was also a lot more respectable and better behaved than the wannabe bad boys that were crawling all over the place.

As you'll remember I mentioned Jessie before, he had stepped in and saved Matt from being stabbed back at Klute. In the time I worked with Jessie I never had an issue with him, on a couple of occasions we talked after he had over reacted with a couple of the guys. Jessie had a short temper and would jump into the fights with you if he was nearby and you had to respect a manager that would do that for you. We're still friends to this day.

Whilst briefly back at Penthouse I had a call from Stefan my friend at Klute. They had decided to get rid of the guys they brought in, make him the head doorman and he had inquired if myself and Dom would like to come back.

So a meeting was set up.....

ADDICTED TO THE LIFE

New Name Same Game

So the meeting with Dom and I was set up. We turned up at the club now under the name Bonsai. We sat down in a booth opposite Stefan, Nigel our old boss, Matt the Greek who was now the manager and Jim – if you remember way back at the beginning of the book Jim and I had a bit of a history of run ins from back in the days at V.

So we sit and listen to Nigel talking about what would be expected if we were to come back, he lays it on pretty thick and then he asks if we have anything to say? I looked at Dom and decided I would be best at handling the response. I pointed out that neither I nor Dom had asked for this meeting, it was you guys that had called us and not the other way around. This did kind of put the kybosh on Nigel's speech.

Dom had no problem with working at Bonsai or with Stefan again, but he was working at Halo – used to be known as V – and was not in the mood to come back as he had a nice set up there. I other hand was interested in coming back as Penthouse was just as much trouble as it had ever been. I pointed out that I had no problem working for Stefan as head door, I didn't know Matt but hadn't heard anything back about him, I had no problem with Nigel and then it got to Jim. We just looked at each other. I said "well we certainly go back a long way." We both laughed and expressed there were no hard feelings. I pointed out that in a few weeks I would be going to university in London, but I could work until that point.

The shifts at Bonsai were uneventful and my last few weeks in Bournemouth in the clubbing scene were not book worthy, however...... back to the horrible misadventures in my spare time.

That is a lot! I mean for one person that really is a lot. From the right angle you could ski down it or just do a classic Tony Montana moment in it. I just looked at it and it didn't even really phase me. It was an entire shoe box of cocaine and it was mine. I hadn't got it to share or sell, it was specifically for me. My own personal use, you would think that something in my mind would twig, when your personally party supply goes from a couple of bags to a shoe box then maybe, just maybe you might have an issue that needs dealing with.

So one night I don't have much going on. I messaged a few girls from Penthouse and see if any of them want to come by after work - who else are you going to call at 3am?

A few of the girls came over and I whacked out my party box. By 6am most had fallen by the waste side. It was just me and one of the girls left standing. However we didn't end up standing for long. Maddison and I ended up in my box room. One thing I learnt was that she was a squirter! Literally a bucket at a time! Things did however get a little awkward. Now I'm used to seeing some rough stuff in the bedroom, but what happened next caught even me off guard.

So we're hitting the final run and the water works start again, however this time around something is different. I look down and in front of me is, well there's no nice way to

COCAINE COMBAT

ADDICTED TO THE LIFE

put this, it's shit, a piece of human shit. I try my best to keep focus and hard and as I'm manoeuvring around I get some tissue round the item in question and move it out the way. Whilst continuing it dawns on me I haven't moved it far enough as just as she moves over, she flips the duvet and the shit ends up being flung up the wall.

I'm trying my best to keep momentum working away from behind, but I can't help but stare at this shit just sliding down the wall inch by inch. Luckily when on the job I am incredibly focused. We managed to finish round two and have quick grind on the kitchen table before she left.

The next day I walked into Lloyd's room and ask if he has any industrial strength cleaning products? He asks why and I say in my defence it wasn't me. He comes into my room and asks what the fuck happened and I tell him it wasn't me. To this day there is still a pale streak running down the wall where the paint and shit used to be.

A few weeks later just before I was due to leave for university it was my birthday. I went on an absolutely mammoth bender with enough coke to ski down. It culminated with me having a few hours sleep and having to freshen up on route to meet my brother and mother at my Nan's for my birthday celebration.

I drive off and my phone was pinging with messages. I checked through some and then just cruised along to the radio. It was at that moment that Maroon 5 came on, this was the music that had pretty much summed up mine and Charlottes relationship. Every time we had a problem or something come up, they released a song that seemed to correlate with what was going on with us. My phone pinged again and I checked the message, it was from Charlotte wishing me a happy birthday. It had been a while since we had spoken and the last conversation hadn't been that pleasant on my end.

I was sat in four lanes of traffic and just broke down. I just sobbed uncontrollably in my car, traffic built up behind me, but I couldn't fucking move, I just couldn't function. I was on the come down from hell and all the stuff I had been blocking out for the last few months with all the drugs and alcohol and partying I suddenly couldn't keep at bay any longer. I eventually got moving and pulled into a lay by just off the road side and just carried on crying. I rang my uncle Marky, he had battled his own personal demons when it came to alcohol and he had taken me to some meetings to see if they would help me out. He was so nice when he spoke to me, he just let me talk, get it out and then he told me it was ok to cry, it didn't make me less of a man, it just meant I had been trying to deal with too much and it was overwhelming. He told me he'd had a cry the other day, he just sat down on a bench whilst out for a walk and had a little weep.

After that I got a call from the bromance and he had a little chat with me and told me it was alright. After some time I got myself together and carried on my drive. I arrived nearly an hour late and didn't look that good. My mum asked if I was ok and I told her what had happened on the way over and she seemed very concerned, I talked and put her at ease and we carried on with my birthday lunch.

ADDICTED TO THE LIFE

So the time had come to go to university. I packed up my stuff at Lloyds and my friend Gay Dave – he wasn't really gay – came over. He had offered to look after my dog Freddy for a short term whilst I made other arrangements. I burst into tears saying goodbye to Freddy, he had been with me through some of the hardest parts of my life and now I was about to lose him. He looked so confused at what was happening and I just cried and in the end Dave just had to take him outside as I couldn't even talk to say goodbye to him.

The next day my dad picked me up and dropped me off to my new home in London.

Going to University and getting away from things was probably a great idea, but it would have been better if I had gone and got some sort of professional help (again) and actually been in a proper facility to help me out. I was mentally shot to bits and incredibly fragile and unstable.

ADDICTED TO THE LIFE

New Beginnings or so we thought

To say my transition up into student living was not a smooth one would have been an understatement! The drive up with my dad was odd. He asked me how I felt and I genuinely had to keep my crying back. I needed a break away from everything that was going on, but I think more than anything I needed to go back into a treatment programme.

I turned up at my uni house and was less than underwhelmed. There had been a problem with my application. A late payment lost my place on campus and I ended up in a house about a 30 minute walk from the campus. My dad helped unload the very minimal belongings I had and then headed on back home to Bournemouth.

I was living with two other guys and they were nice enough, but they literally lived in their rooms, playing Xbox and didn't come down to socialise at all. I had missed the window a month or so earlier to pay my deposit for my student accommodation and live on campus with the majority of the students, but as I called a day late they gave away my spot and told me I was not a priority in finding another place as technically I had 'rejected' the accommodation offer by not paying. I eventually found a house about a 30/40 minute walk from the campus in the opposite direction to the town centre and all the places the majority of the students went to.

Fresher's week is supposed to be the week where everyone goes out and gets on it, makes new friends and pretty much fucks anything that moves. I however was based off campus and no one posted anything to you about events. I spent my time in the lounge on my own and when left alone things for me don't go well. I couldn't find a dealer in the area and didn't know who to approach, so I went back to what I knew from the beginning. I drank solidly and popped pain killers all throughout the day and into the early hours of the morning.

I managed to get down to the campus to find out what was going on with my course and when my schedule would start. I was stood in the university office and as I went to walk out some guy muttered something as I went past. I turned and asked what they said and it was one of the rugby league team. He said "you look mean, you fancy playing rugby league?" As time would go on, this guy would be one of my good friends at university, he was called Floppy – that's a name not me describing his man hood.

I went to the fresher's fare and signed up to play rugby league. I also managed to speak to one of the guys who were doing security and he put me in contact with his boss and I got a job bouncing at a club in town. Different city, but same routine.

My course was interesting, but it was pretty obvious from the beginning that there was definitely an age difference between me and everyone else there. I was about 8/9 years older than anyone else, bar a couple of people. I only had a couple of classes per week and the rest of my time was just spent on the sofa in the lounge slowly numbing myself to the world again with pain killers and alcohol. Luckily my shifts at the new venue started and that gave me something to do.

ADDICTED TO THE LIFE

I was working at Liquid in the town centre. It was a massive 3 floor night club. You came through a really long walk way leading into the first club room, this played RnB and hip hop, up some stairs and you went into a massive open dance floor, a bar on either side, if you looked behind you then saw the 3rd floor VIP bar and seating area and then down a corridor behind that and up another flight of stairs was the smoking area and the toilets. It was a big venue and had a large team working it.

Wednesday nights were student night, so I saw loads of people from campus and on my course, Friday and Saturday were open to anyone.

I did begin training with the rugby league team and played in my first nines tournament, which then ended in me dislocating my shoulder and fucking up my ligaments. I was in a sling for a week and couldn't train or lift weight or work the doors for a few weeks. What else was there to do, but sink further into my old habits? I chain smoked, drank and popped pills all the time. I had moved away from all my friends and brought all of my problems with me.

One night at the club a fight broke out and I ran over to see a group of fully grown men attacking one of the students from the uni. They had mistaken him for some random guy that apparently had an issue with one of their friends' sisters and ended up with them kicking the student in the face knocking out his front tooth. Fun fact the next year at uni we ended up living together. We hit the Christmas break and I had never been so keen to get back to Bournemouth. I got off the train, dropped my stuff at my dad's and headed straight into town to see the guys. I met Alex and Lloyd and few of the other guys at the Christmas bar in town and proceeded to drink and order as much coke as I could. This was essentially how my Christmas break went whilst I was back home. I didn't want to go back to London, I wanted to be back where I knew people, and I wanted to be back with the people I knew. The problem was I wasn't really back; I was still on a continual cycle of drugs and just had no real grasp on reality. I may have been in the room, but I wasn't on the planet.

During Christmas break my mum talked to me and encouraged me to go back. She pretty much explained that I had absolutely nothing here. If I went back, then I might have a chance at doing something with my life. I had never hidden what I did from my mum, she knew how I made money for so many years and she knew that I used a lot and she was genuinely terrified that any day she would get a call from the police or my brother or dad having to explain to her that I was gone – either in prison or more likely dead.

Begrudgingly I went back to give it one last go.

Things got a bit better in the second half. The other students had got a bit more relaxed and started being friendlier with each other. They saw me on nights out and the girls would all come running up to me, I was like a novelty to them I think.

One thing I did manage to bring back up to London with me was steroids. I managed to pick up a supply to get me through the rest of the year. I lived in the gym now my shoulder was healed.

COCAINE COMBAT

ADDICTED TO THE LIFE

Life at the club was the same as any other. The people were exactly the same. Only difference is, when you work the door the Bournemouth you hear "I'm from London bruv" and in London you hear "do you know what part of London I'm from bruv?"

You know what else never changes in night clubs? The girls. I was working in liquid and some girls who worked at the Liquid in Slough, the next town over would come in every Wednesday night and drink and party. Just so happens one of them takes a shine to me and after a couple of weeks we get talking. Now by talking I mean I'm working and she is shit faced babbling at me – just like in Romeo and Juliet.

One Wednesday night as I'm leaving the club, she happens to still be outside with her friends. I'm smoking fag and waiting for my taxi when she comes up to talk to me. Her and her friends are having some sort of debate over the taxi fare. Now before I go any further I suppose a little more of an accurate description of this girl may help to set the tone for what is about to happen with the rest of this story. She has bleach blonde hair, big hoop earrings and has her hand bag on the floor, because "when she kicks off, she gets fighty and her mates know it" I know, I know I do attractive the classiest of ladies.

My taxi pulls up and I tell her if she has any issues then just give me a buzz. An hour later I get a message from her saying her friends have all left her and she's sitting in an underground passage with no way to get home. So I order a taxi and go collect her and bring her back to mine – I'm not paying to take her ass all the way to Slough and then come back to my house on my own.

We get back to mine and I go into the bathroom, she goes into my room and gets herself comfy. I come back in thinking well at least tonight has not been a total loss. I come back into my room and nearly fucking go arse over tit on this pile on my floor. I steady myself and check what the fuck I have just tripped on. I examine the pile and sift through each item, there are heels, tights, hair, nails, chicken fillets and eye lashes. First off I think this girl had somehow melted at the excitement of getting to sleep with me. I check the bed and there appears to be someone in it, so that's the first theory out the window. I flick back the covers and to my surprise it appears in the time I've gone for a piss she has morphed from a 19 yr old girl into an 8 yr old flat chested boy. I still did it. I even paid for her taxi home the next day – always the gentleman. She did leave me with a little reminder of our dalliance together. I was probably the only 27 year old in university history that had to try to hide a hickey from his classmates – it was spotted and it was mentioned by a lot of people.

I was working the basement room at Liquid and a fight breaks out. I see two absolute gimps throwing hand bags – that's a metaphor for awful punches and not actual hand bags - and doing a lot of vocal gesturing. I break up the incident and one guy is struggling and trying to fight me. Quick hip toss to the floor and he's no longer giving it the big man. Another fight breaks out 5 fucking feet from me, so I jump up and leave the guy restrained by another doorman. I separate the new retards and suddenly something hits me from behind. I don't mean a punch, I mean like a whole body. I was partially bent over and the dickhead from earlier has got himself up and tried to jump me from behind, but he's jumped nearly

ADDICTED TO THE LIFE

clean over and clipped my mouth with his trailing arm. I'm looking up and behind me wondering what had happened and then I look down to see this guy lying on his back like a turtle unable to get up. I drop a knee on his chest and then drag his ass out of the club. The police turn up and take the guy away. They ask me to come down to the station and fill out an incident report and point out that since there's evidence to support he talked me from behind and caused an injury – cut my lip – I could be entitled to compensation. I remember sitting in that Perspex booth they have in there, being talked to through some microphone system and thinking I do not want to be back in here for any reason any time soon.

So university was actually starting to go my way and I was finding a rhythm there. Then one night it hit an inevitable speed bump.

So I'm working at Liquid and everything is pretty much like any other night. All of a sudden we get a code red call to the VIP booths. I come sprinting up from Envy, the first dance room and up the stairs into the mix. All hell has broken loose up there. I'm greeted by a sea of customers all fighting and bundling into each other. I don't know what's happened to cause this, but it's pretty much every customer in the club going for the door team. I grab one of the bodies whose currently trying to attack one of the door staff and drag him through the very narrow corridor leading up towards the back exit. Unfortunately, but not surprisingly we get jammed in due to the amount of bodies. Both my arms are locked around my guy and there is some dickhead thumping me repeatedly in the back of the head. I'm unable to get him to stop, but I manage to turn my head and get a good look at him. Eventually we get through the bottle neck and out down the fire exit/back stairway to get my guy out the front door and away from the club.

After the front door has calmed down, one of the bar supervisors tells me the guy who was hitting me is upstairs in the smoking area. I go back in and up the back stair way and as I swing open the fire doors guess who is stood with his back to me still running his mouth off about what's just happened? Yeah you guessed it, it's my happy slapper. I grab him by the back of the neck and pull him through the fire doors.

Now I maintain that he struggled with me and I restrained him as best as I could, but he struggled repeatedly and took a bit of a tumble, but eventually was manoeuvred out of the club by one of the managers and me.

I don't give much thought to the incident and head home to Bournemouth to Easter. I bought myself a motor to get around in and decided that it would nice to visit my mum for a couple of days as I hadn't seen her for a while.

I'm sat at my dad's and my mobile goes off. It's 9pm, it's a Thursday night and I'm not expecting any calls. A withheld number normally means only one thing and that's the police. My dad tells me to answer and I tell him it'll be the police, but he says just answer it so I do. No prizes for guessing, it is the police. Apparently the guy I had brought out of the club after the huge brawl has gone and filed charges against me.

COCAINE COMBAT

ADDICTED TO THE LIFE

The officer on the phone asks where I am as I was not at my registered address. I ask what he means my registered address; I was not aware I had registered with the police??? He informs me that they sent officers to the club to get my details and then sent a car to my address, but I wasn't home.

I inform the officer where I am and that I will happily come in and answer any questions when I come back to London in a few days. The next morning I go off to visit my mum and don't think any more about the phone call. My mum lives way out in the country and you cannot get reception for love or money.

After a couple of days I get back to my dad's. He is less than pleased to see me. He informs me that whilst I was away the police sent multiple units round to try and find me. They had left a card with a contact number for me to call as soon as I got back. My dad had told them the first time they came round that I was at my mums and that since they divorced over a decade ago he did not know her address or had much contact with her. They assumed he was lying and sent round a further 3 units at different points over the two days I was gone.

I called the number on the card and asked why they had sent units round to my dad's house. They simply stated they had wished to talk to me and I stated that we had agreed I would travel back after a couple days and speak to them and that they had not insisted it was that urgent and they had no right in continually harassing my dad. They did apologise for that after I pointed out that it was his house and having multiple police units pull up was embarrassing in front of his neighbours, and also bordering on harassment of a near 60 year old man.

I was informed that I was to appear at the police station back in Uxbridge by 2:30pm Saturday afternoon or a warrant would be issued for my arrest. I was now aware I was in more trouble than I had initially thought. The guy from the club had filed charges and was threatening to sue the police. Apparently after he was ejected he tried to get an officer to come and arrest me, the officer was informed he was involved in the fighting upstairs inside the club and had been sent on his way.

However the young man was apparently not in a good way. He went to the hospital and was diagnosed with a fractured eye socket, broken cheek bone and other further defence wounds throughout his body.

I got up on Saturday morning and packed my stuff up. I was still on Easter break and was supposed to be spending that time at my dad's. I told my dad if he didn't hear anything from me by about 5pm then he should assume the worst and that I wouldn't be coming home that evening.

I will never forget the genuine look of despair on his face as I pulled out the drive way. My dad had heard about me being in trouble before. He had already seen me deal with charges before, but I think even he realised this was more serious than the others and was possibly going to be finding myself off on a little vacation.

ADDICTED TO THE LIFE

I made the drive up on my own. I parked up at my house in Uxbridge and caught the bus into town. I didn't want to park my car in town as I didn't know what was going to happen when I got in the station.

I got to the station with about 30 minutes to spare and there was queue of people. I sat on a chair and waited for the queue to die down. After about 40 minutes someone came over and asked what I was waiting for. I told her I had been asked to come in and gave her my name. She told me to wait there and off she went through some doors.

So I'm sat there waiting and the doors swing open. Two officers come out and stand themselves either side of me. A few moments later and another officer come out and asks me stand up and follow him through. I walk through with personal escort and am lead to a holding cell. Apparently they've had to convert this for our interview as all the other rooms are occupied. I walk in and am greeted by two detectives, a stack of folders and some video equipment. I get the feeling they are very prepared for my arrival.

The second I sat down it dawned on me how serious this was compared to the last time I had been brought in and my arsehole was going 50p 20p the whole time! They asked if I wanted to wait for legal representation and I said I was ok but knew that I had the right to request a solicitor at any point during the interview.

They present me with the information supplied by the gentleman who has alleged the offences against me. They repeated to me the version of events that they had been told according to my accuser and then asked me to give my side of events.

He had stated that I had attacked him in a frenzied attack, repeatedly choked him unconscious and struck him whilst he was unable to properly defend himself and that had resulted in the more severe injuries he suffered to his face.

I gave my side of the events. He had tried to fight me in the stair way and I had given him the option to walk down the stairs and out quietly to avoid any incidents. He had wrestled with me and may have hit his head during the struggle, but I couldn't 100% sure. I did mention that I believed that the injuries he had suffered had been a direct result to him being involved in the mass brawl prior to his removal from the club.

The detectives listened to my version of the events and informed I had the right to legal representation again. They then began to play the video footage collected from the night club. They had 13 cameras to view. We went through each of the cameras and as we went through each one and the first few showed nothing. As we began to go through more of the cameras they also showed nothing, we slowly counted down the last few cameras. Camera 10 nothing, camera 11 nothing, camera 12 nothing and camera 13 nothing.

I looked at the detective as he turned off the TV and he looked back at me. I sat there without saying anything and waited to see what was next. He shuffled some files and then said based on the evidence in front of them they would have to drop all charges due to a lack of evidence. I was so relieved, this whole saga had literally been a fishing expedition for them to try and get me to confess before we got to the video tapes and their lack of footage. I

ADDICTED TO THE LIFE

walked out and let out a huge sigh of relief the second I stepped outside. I turned around to see the two detectives looking at me; I just smiled and walked off into the sunset. I got back to my car and headed back to Bournemouth to enjoy the rest of my Easter break.

ADDICTED TO THE LIFE

Summer fun

      My first year at university ended without incident- other than the trip to talk to the police – and it was time to head back to home to Bournemouth.

      Fortunately before I left I had managed to sort out some more convenient accommodation. I got a room at a house a few hundred yards from the campus and with one of the guys from the rugby league team – Neo. We had got on together on nights out and the house was insanely cheap compared to other accommodation I had tried to find. I was paying literally less than half of what everyone else in the area was paying. So things were already looking better than before.

      During my time at university I had developed an interest in barbering and had been going to my mate Kaz barbershop. You remember Kaz from way back in the start of the book? Yeah this was the same guy, he had a new business and took me in and began teaching me to cut hair. I balanced this out with working at Halo in the evenings.

      Halo was what used to be V. If you remember, it had been closed down due to a stabbing and was then bought and reopened by new owners, one of whom was an old face from the clubbing scene, my Ty. Ty was one of the faces from the clubbing scene for the past few years, in the nicest way he came off as a shady fucker, but he had bought into the new club and he worked his ass off to prove that he knew what he was doing with the club and that he was a credible businessman. In all honesty we were not the closest of mates, we knew each other from the nightclub world and some other mutual interests, but I couldn't really fault working at Halo under his ownership. He carried himself as businessman and did everything he could to make the place a success. The opening hours were the same and I could make decent money whilst training with Kaz. I didn't get paid to learn at Kaz shop, but the guy paid for everything when I was there, he bought me lunch and snacks every day. You couldn't fault his generosity when it came to people.

      I was having a good time back in Bournemouth. The club was fun and I was working with some old friends from before, there was Dom, Jordan and Chris from Klute, Lloyd from the Mary Shelly and Harlan who I would work with during my brief return stints at V. There were also a couple of new faces that I hadn't seen before.

      My first shift I turned up and started talking with Church the head door, we had met briefly at a couple of other clubs when I had done some extra cash shifts, he knew how I worked and was happy to have me there. The agreement was essentially that I was there to join Dom and Jordan inside and deal with the fights and more physical altercations as that seemed to be the most persistent problem – well the most persistent problem was that other than a couple guys the door team just didn't have a much of a clue in what it was doing and just didn't work together.

      A large stag group began coming through the club doors and I was stood with a female doorman called Sarah. This was her first club and her first stint as a bouncer. She had

ADDICTED TO THE LIFE

little to zero people skills and the second this group walked in, she turned to me and said you're searching them. As they came in I counted how many of them there were and stopped them as they came through. I asked them to pick a number and the first one said the number, I stopped the person that corresponded with that number and said congratulations you've been selected for a random search, so you have 3 seconds to either get rid of any drugs you have or shove them so far up your arse I don't want to find them.

Sarah seemed shocked that I had said this and repeated it to Church so many times. I'm guessing she was trying to get me in trouble or make herself look good for whatever reason. I'll take the time to explain it now. I said that to that group because they were a large group of males with the possibility to get rowdy when they were in the club. Now by having a laugh and joke with them as they came in I had established a bit of a rapport with them and therefore if something did happen in the club and they were involved it would be easier for me to deal with them as they would associate me with having a bit of banter with them as they came in. This tactic is pretty handy especially when you have members of your door team who are going to be next to useless and have already shown they are happy to avoid any type of conflict.

Obviously a long with nightclub work came ladies and staff socials. Halo had one every now and again on a Wednesday night. I would go to them, drink, sniff and generally have a good time. The summer had been pretty fun and I was feeling relaxed about heading back to university in September, but first we had to get through my birthday.

It was on a Wednesday, I had the boys out for a meal and then onto Cameo for drinking and shenanigans. I had had some trouble sleeping and one of the guys from the gym had given me some medical grade muscle relaxants he had left over from his surgery. These were very helpful for when you had done too much coke and were a bit too wired to sleep.

So we're out for my birthday and I'm having a good time, I'm drinking and there is an abundance of guys with coke on them – usual case at any party I'm involved in. I'm drinking away and chatting to some random short bird who happens to be in the club when my friend Lauren comes up to me and says "talk to whoever you want, but take Sophie home." I hadn't really given it much thought, she was one of the girls who worked behind the bar and we had never really chatted, but hey ho it was my birthday and guaranteed bang is always a good icing on the cake.

I left the club with Sophie having not really said more than a few words to her. We got back to mine and I went into the bathroom, got sorted and then joined her in my bed. I was pretty impressed at my ability to keep a hard on with the amount of coke I had done. After round one was done I thought I would probably need to get some sleep, so I popped a muscle relaxant and tried to nod off. Apparently this wasn't an option as someone wanted round two. I'd like to say I leapt up and like sturdy mountain lion roared and went dominated her, but thanks to the muscle relaxant I was more like a drunk slug with a hard on slamming into a wall.

ADDICTED TO THE LIFE

I hadn't really timed taking the relaxant well. They last for about 12 hours and I had taken mine at around 5am. My brother woke me at 10am saying I needed to get up and ready to meet mum and Nan for lunch at 12 – you can see the timing issue here!

I woke up Sophie and managed to pull some clothes on. I was still unable to move properly let alone drive, so I got my brother to drive my car whilst I lay on the passenger chair like a drunken slug. We dropped Sophie off and made our way to meet my mum and Nan for lunch.

I came staggering into the pub and sat down at the table with my mum and Nan and you could tell that the lights were on but no one was home. I told my mum I was off my tits on muscle relaxants and she laughed, my Nan said she had never seen me look so calm and relaxed.

We got back to my nans for my traditional birthday cake and there are still videos on my Facebook of me falling out of the chair as I try to blow out my birthday candles. It was an interesting birthday.

Here's the funny thing about how random things can get. I was finishing up early at the club and got talking to Amber who was apparently Sophie's best mate. We had a chat and I made a joke about shagging her and she then said it would never happen. Fast forward two hours later and I can tell you what her vagina tastes like. The second a girl says she's not interested they instantly become more desirable.

Now literally in my last week at Halo I got talking to one of the girls who were hired to dance at the club between 12-2am. I finished my last week and headed back up to university.

COCAINE COMBAT

ADDICTED TO THE LIFE

The second coming

So as I stated literally the second I had to move to back up to London I got chatting to Lucy one of the dancers at the club. We ended up talking over Facebook – that old cliché –as I was in one part of the country she was in the other. Now I knew absolutely nothing about her, I had never met her before Halo and I had never met or heard about her in any other club I had worked at. I knew she had a young daughter because she told me – I'll take a moment to pay a compliment that is most definitely due. Her daughter was only a few months old and if you looked at Lucy you would never have even guessed she had ever even been in a room with a child let alone recently given birth. For all you mums who say they are carrying baby weight years later, I call bullshit! – Otherwise I would never have guessed. As I couldn't just pop down the street and take her out, I thought the nice thing to do would be to send her some flowers. If I had learnt anything from my relationship with Charlotte it was that little gestures would go a long way. I messaged her friend Charlie and asked what her favourite flowers were and for her address, Charlie thought it was very cute and gave me the information I needed and I sent the flowers off.

I got a message on Facebook later the next day saying she had received the flowers and chocolates and it had taken her a bit to figure out they were from me. She said it was a shame I couldn't be there so I made arrangements and on Friday night I travelled down to see her.

We met up a couple of times over the weekend whilst out in town. I'll be honest I really was not prepared for what was to come. For some reason people just seemed to go fucking mad at the fact we had been seen out together and that something was going on between us.

I went back up to London and for the next week was berated with messages gossiping about her, the funny thing was the same people who were messaging me saying shit about her, were talking to her and saying shit about me. This was relentless for two weeks and the onslaught of it all just meant it was far too much drama for us to even have a conversation let alone go for a drink or out to dinner. So the only thing was to just let it go and carry on with our individual lives. I have never been in a situation that generated that much gossip and attention, it was like being a fucking celebrity. I'll say it's a shame because she was generally fun to talk and seemed like a very nice and genuine person, but hey ho onwards and upwards.

Living at the hill – as our house was commonly known – was a good laugh, the guys were all very relaxed and everyone got on well. My course was looking good and I was training like a machine in the gym again. Things in general were going pretty well. I actually played an entire season without getting injured. I got up to Christmas without any incident at either of the clubs I was working at. I did Friday nights at the club on campus as Friday night was student night. People had begun to recognise me on campus; I was lovingly referred to as that scary, jacked guy who did theatre. Saturday nights I was generally back over at Liquid.

ADDICTED TO THE LIFE

Uni this time was banging. I and the rugby team were having a blinding season and I had managed to remain injury free, I wasn't using coke when I was there, the team socials were always a good time and I tried to go out on those more. It was always entertaining doing the Friday night at the student club on campus because I would see all the rugby boys out and the people off the course – it's always fun being the doorman and watching your friends make drunken mistakes that you'll get to remind them about the next day.

As Christmas break loomed I began to unwind as I was going to be heading back to Bournemouth again and so far I had managed to avoid any legal issues or big incidents.

I was working at the uni club and everything had gone pretty smoothly. The night had ended incident free and then I got a call outside. One of my housemates James – the one who had his teeth kicked out the year before – as he's having an incident with some of the university football team. Apparently some girl has said something in the club and it's all kicked off outside. Looking at about 7 of the football all crowding my housemate. I go in and defuse the situation and James and two of his friends head through campus towards our house and I go back inside.

When I'm inside the queue for the cloakroom is getting busy and people are pushing and shoving. One guy keeps shoving people, I tell him to pack it the fuck in and I'm not in the mood. He starts shoving a girl in front of him, so I tell to get the fuck out! I give him a nudge in the direction of the door and he lunges back swinging a wild haymaker at me. I duck and put the guy in a choke hold and move him out the club. He keeps struggling and starts scratching at my face. I tell him stop or shits going to get unpleasant. He carries on, so I put my fingers up his nose and yank upwards. A quick sharp pain and he stops struggling. We get outside and I let him go. He comes running back at me and I side step and drop him to the floor again. He gives me the trusted "in my country you'd be dead."

Whilst dealing with that muppet which delayed me getting home, the football team members who had been arguing with my mate had followed him home and attacked him and his two mates a few hundred yards before our house. I came home to a housemate covered in blood and bruises. I messaged the boys at uni who knew the football team and said I wanted the name of everyone involved. The next day I got the names of all of them and then got messages from them all blaming someone else or claiming they hadn't followed my friend home. Needless to say it's amazing how quickly guys go from hard man in a group to the biggest pussies on planet earth. I offered each one of them the chance at a one on one with me to settle it and all of them declined. Eventually my mate asked me to drop it, but there's still one lanky, blonde cunt that has definitely got a meeting with me when the opportunity strikes. Yeah I'm talking to you Liam you fucking coward.

The next Monday I was in Costa on campus – my usual place of business – when the guy from the Friday night incident at the cloakroom comes in. He's got his nose all bandaged up. He looks over at me and I smile back and wave, he turns around and leaves the coffee shop.

I had decided that I would avoid club work after all the drama with people over the Lucy incident. I wasn't about to go back to a club where the people I was supposed to be friends with had been talking shit about me.

COCAINE COMBAT

ADDICTED TO THE LIFE

The funny thing now is that a problem had apparently developed between me and the new manager at Halo Dan. He had previously dated Lucy and had made some remarks about me. Now I didn't really give a shit about him or his opinion. However, people were questioning me as a man. Now it sounds silly, but when people start questioning if you've got the balls then in my areas of work that can cause an issue. People will begin to think they can take the piss and in door work that can be problematic, but with my side business that can be an absolute nightmare and it's just something you can't have.

I thought the best thing to do was call Scott for advice, he was still in Bournemouth and I knew I could count on him for the right kind of advice. He had heard what had been said and advised that something needed to be done. He said that I wasn't to use anything but cash, I wasn't to make any plans for transport, he would drive up and get me, I would stay with him and not tell anyone I was back in town and then we would simply wait for when Dan finished his shift one night and then come see him at his flat and have a 'discussion.' I'm not saying it was something that we had previous experience of, but it certainly was not a spur of the moment idea that just suddenly came to us like a vision from Jesus.

I arrived back in Bournemouth and bumped into a good friend of mine. He had just incurred a massive problem. On a night out he was involved in a very serious incident and as it turns out Dan was going to be a key witness for his defence when it came to court. He was aware that there was an issue between us and I knew him well enough to discuss the issue and how it was going to be dealt with.

Now like I said myself and the person in question go back a very long way and have other business interests that are mutually beneficial to us keeping a good relationship. He asked me as a personal favour and asked that I would delay my plans until after his court date. After that I would be free to do whatever I pleased and he would even throw me a bonus as a way of thanking me for my patience. I agreed to put my plans on hold until he had what he needed.

The court proceedings were strung out for several more months due to delays and in all honesty by the time his business was concluded I couldn't be arsed with Dan anymore. I had gotten a good deal from the delay and more importantly I had moved on by then, my focus was fixed on other things.

After Christmas I had gotten involved in an MMA event as ring announcer. I did the job for my old trainer and friend Jordan at his new Showtime MMA organisation and doing that job for them actually lead me to the offer of a paid gig for another boxing promotion that had started up.

Just after Christmas I was struck with some unfortunate and truly saddening news. A friend of mine from the world of door work had been battling cancer and sadly just when it looked like he had fought through it, he suffered a stroke that inevitably took his life. I was sitting in bed with a girl called Roxanne when I got the message. My dirty mid week escape had suddenly taken a truly sad turn.

ADDICTED TO THE LIFE

I came back to Bournemouth to work on Total Collision the boxing promotion that had hired me as an MC. The event itself was big; Ilker had gotten involved in the promotion of the event and put his knowledge of the promotions and marketing game he had learnt from 20 years of clubbing experience on it. I met Paul who was one of the main guys who was responsible for putting the show on. And the other half of the operation was Khalid, Taz cousin who I knew from the nightclub scene from years back.

The show was busy and I pretty much took over running the ringside area. I organised everything to make it as easy as possible for the DJ and all the runners and helped it run as smoothly as possible. It was a long night!

A couple of weeks later I headed back into Bournemouth and had a meeting with Paul and Ilker about the event. I had brought a number of ideas that would help make the event easier to run both behind the scenes and front of house. They were impressed and brought me in as an event manager – I got an upgrade.

At the next event I got to witness former world champion Steve Collins sing to a sold out event in an attempt to stop the crowd brawl that had broken out.... It was an interesting sight. I'll give you the story just so you can really appreciate what happened.

So on the card as the co-main event we have two guys who seem to absolutely hate each other. I have no idea what started their 'beef' and I didn't care. All I knew was it made good ticket sales and that meant good business. Now Jake has a rather large following in the crowd and there are a few handy little numbers amongst them and a lot of mouth pieces. Now on the card as well we have a few boys representing the travelling community and they always bring a fucking huge following – proper travellers take great pride in fighting and they come out as a whole community to support each other. Jakes following are round one side of the ring and running next to them are the 120 or so traveller supporters. Now a bit of spat breaks out with Jakes boys and the traveller fans and it looks like its set to be a fucking blood bath. In all honesty had it kicked off the travellers would have buried those boys without a fucking doubt. Hence the sudden singing by Steve Collins to help calm the crowd. Oh and for those wondering Jake won the fight by decision in a very well fought bout.

COCAINE COMBAT

ADDICTED TO THE LIFE

Fallen Warriors

Towards the end of my second year of university I was struck with the most devastating news I had received in years.

I was back at my dad's during Easter break when I got a message from Scott saying big Dave had passed. He hadn't responded to his work colleague knocking on his door. I thought this was just a mix up and told them just knock louder and say you have chicken. Scott text back and said it wasn't a wind up. I jumped into my car and drove round to his house and met Scott, Lee and LJ who were waiting down in the car park.

We all just stood there in the car park. No one was saying anything, everyone just looked so down. I didn't know what to do so I just said the first thing that came into my head, "I hope they don't check his laptop and find all that turreted porn he's downloaded." The boys all laughed and it broke the mood.

We just waited in the car park for the police to finish their investigation. The problem with Dave was he was a huge guy and he lived on the first floor of a flat with a spiral staircase at the entrance. The coroner couldn't bring him down on his own. So the only thing to do was have me and the guys help. We joked it was the one time we all did cardio together.

It marked the fourth person I had known on the doors who had died in the last three years; Big Stevie G, Matt, Simon and then Big Dave. All of them were taken tragically and sudden and all long before their time.

Dave's funeral was by far the hardest thing I ever had to do and it took me a long time to get over. To this day I still break down at random times when he pops into my head, I wasn't ready to say goodbye to him and I'm still not. He was my go to guy for advice with my problems. He had beaten his personal demons years previously and come through the other side a much better person. The funeral day itself was a lovely occasion or as lovely as one can be. Everyone who could make it went. It was held in a small village near his parents and they were truly overwhelmed at the level of love and respect people had for Dave.

The only dampener was the behaviour of Leigh who couldn't keep his mouth shut about some personal issues he and Chris had. Swearing and show booting in the line to speak to Dave's parents as they were trying to thank everyone who had come out to pay respects and say farewell to Dave. Leigh you're a narsacistic, selfish prick and your behaviour was disgusting...Got an issue with that, then you come see me any fucking time and I will slap the stupid out of your fucking mouth.

Losing Dave came at such an unexpected time and the loss literally broke my heart. I became ill trying to deal with it and when I went to the doctors for tests to help find out why I had been feeling so ill, they clocked my blood pressure at over 190 and realised that the symptoms of fatigue I had been suffering with were most likely stress on my heart from

ADDICTED TO THE LIFE

having to deal with this situation. We monitored my heart rate and for six weeks it never went below 180.

I'm going to take a moment here to talk about something else that also falls into this realm.

There is a campaign that has been running on Facebook for years and it's to do with two friends of mine Peter and Karl Mallon. When I was finishing my college course, they went through a rough patch, their parents had decided to separate and to give them one nice memory before the ensuing unpleasantness of what was to come. Their father Steve wanted to take them and some of their friends on holiday in Spain.

During this holiday tragedy struck. Whilst in a Spanish bar the boys got into an altercation with some of the locals. They were outnumbered by about 15 to 5 I think. During this attack their father was killed. Whilst trying to defend his sons some of the group of locals ganged up on Steve and threw him off the balcony to his impending death.

Those poor boys not only had to witness the murder of their father but also relay the news back home. For years their fathers' body has sat in a Spanish mortuary whilst this trial continues to be delayed and stalled. They have not been able to bring their father home and say goodbye to him properly.

I am asking anyone who has taken the time to purchase and read this book to go online and show their support and bring their father home where he should be. JUSTICE FOR STEVE MALLON.

ADDICTED TO THE LIFE

The Summer of Sin

I went back to working at Halo as I had done previously. It was a club I knew like the back of my hand and had no problem coming and going to during my split life in London and Bournemouth.

Wouldn't you know it but the Bournemouth football team only went and got promoted. And where did they come to celebrate? Yeah you guessed it, Halo. The club was absolutely rammed the whole night long. When it came to the end of the night getting people out was a nightmare, no one wanted to move and when there are only 7 door staff and 700 people still refusing to leave you know you have to pick your battles carefully.

I am on the top balcony with Lloyd and one of the other guys trying to get drunken, raving football enthusiasts to go downstairs and leave. One particular fan thinks its wise idea to push me, so I shove him straight back and tell him to get the fuck away from away me. He charges at me and I rush him straight back onto one of the seated areas, he's struggling and clawing at my face. I pin him to the booth and squeeze his neck to get him to stop clawing at my face. His mate has very kindly jumped on my back or at least tried to; luckily for me Lloyd has pretty much instantly taken him out of the equation. Now the foolish young man I am dealing with slides his fingers into my mouth – not the smartest move as fingers are fragile and teeth are sharp – I bite down as hard as I can and I can see his eyes water, he's trying to scream, but my hand is locked around his scrawny neck. His body wilts and I release the pressure grip and let his fingers fall out of my mouth. As he is eventually taken out I still have pieces of gristle in my mouth, undoubtedly bits of his finger.

Now the shifts at Halo weren't the only times where my life got interesting over the summer. I did foolishly spend some time putting up with some pre-madonna, coke head bitch that I should have binned off long before, but what can I say, I try to see the good in people.

It did lead to a very interesting first date conversation. She worked as an estate agent in town and told me that her boss had met me before. I said I have no idea who you're boss is and I've never met him. She insisted we had. He was at a birthday party at Aruba and you came in with Taz. He said you were the nutter with gold front teeth. Yeah now that did sound familiar, I did have gold front teeth at one point – you get bored, you have money, you wonder what you'd look like with gold front teeth, so you have them made - The day I finally told her to get fucked I ended up talking to one of the VIP girls from Halo. She was a sweet girl and we went for a drink later that night. Now me being a guy and more accurately an angry and horny fucker I had arranged to meet a girl from tinder later that night as well.

I dropped the nice and pleasant VIP hostess home along with the flowers I had bought her and drove out to the middle of nowhere to meet tinder girl.

I was literally in the middle of nowhere! I pulled up and parked my car by a church and walked up some gravel road to meet her. We walked through what turned out to be a riding school and past a row of caravans. We ended up in the storage shed and I would like to

ADDICTED TO THE LIFE

say it was a wild affair, but truth be told I blew my load in less than 5 minutes and bolted out of there like one of the horses out the blocks at the start of the grand national!

I was quite lucky in that I managed to pull together a string of dates and encounters with a series of really lovely girls over the rest of the summer. I had coffee with a very charming and attractive 20 year old gym enthusiast with a phenomenal ass – I've always been an ass over boob's man. I went on a couple dates and hooked up with a girl I had sort of known before called Bex – fun girl, very dry sense of humour, bit mental but a good ride, but another girl who just changed her mind constantly and turned out to be a waste of time. She did get a free dildo from me as a parting gift. I wonder if when she uses it now she tells her boyfriend where it came from. – and I ended up having one of the most surprising encounters of my life with one of the girls I hadn't seen since I was at Penthouse and worked the Kitty club.

Kittie and I had known each other for years; we got chatting one day just about random stuff. I had seen her out on her birthday whilst I was out having drinks with Bex. We got chatting for a while and arranged to catch up the following night at her place – it was actually all very innocent, just two friends catching up – I went round and spent about seven hours just solidly talking with her and drinking vodka and coke. She was one of the most interesting people I have ever met and she was completely unlike the preconceived concepts you get from people when you just go by how they look (she was an alternative model, covered in tattoos, blonde hair and a chest you could base jump off.) She talked openly and honestly about how work in nightclubs and bars was like putting on a performance. In real life she was quite shy and insecure and seemed to be very similar to me on inside.

One thing leads to another and I ended up having what turned out to be a mini four day adventure with her. To this day she is one of my favourite people to talk to and I think whoever ends up with her will be extremely fortunate!

I was employed for a few months over the summer with a landscaping company and it was ok. It just wasn't for me and I wasn't always in the best of health. As I said earlier the loss of Dave really did affect me and my health. Some days I genuinely had trouble finding the breath to get out of bed, let alone go lug shit around all day. My patience was thin at the best of times and one day I realised that this job was not going to work out.

I was at a job in Ferndown with my boss and it just was not going well. He was already pissed about the amount of work that had been done the day before. I'll say this, I'm the labourer, I lug and move shit. If the guy in charge hasn't laid enough slabs and bricks and I've kept him in muck and supplies all day, then that's his fault not mine.

I've knocked something over and I think it must have been the last straw for Dave my boss as he just starts going off at me and on about everything! He tells me if I want to leave and he'll do the job himself. I sort of zoned out for a bit at that point, my mind just started to try and work things out. I hadn't been spoken to like that in a long time, I do not and will not ever get used to having someone yell at me like I'm a piece of shit. I sized him up and down and he's not a big guy, one solid shot to the chin and he goes down quick and I can just walk

ADDICTED TO THE LIFE

away, but I scan my eye to the right and his mate who owns the house we're working on is stood there and I think he would definitely grass me to the police. So for the first time in ages, I do the smart thing and just take it on the chin and finish the day with Dave. That took a lot of doing. I told Dom about it a couple days later as he worked for Dave as well and he laughed and just said I'm glad you're a bit wiser mate.

ADDICTED TO THE LIFE

On the verge of Gypsy warfare

Halo is busy as fuck and a boxing event has just finished and Shane Cooper and the boys from his Underdogz boxing club had just finished fighting and had booked a table at the club. Now Shane is one of the most respectful guys I have ever met. Whenever he came into the club or I worked with him at one of the boxing events he was always polite and a pleasure to deal with.

Shane and the guys turn up to the club and go through. They have a table upstairs and are busy enjoying their evening. I get a call to the main entrance of the club. Apparently there has been an incident involving one of the guys from Shane's table. I go and find out what's going on. I get shown a picture of CJ one of the guys with Shane and one of the coaches at the boxing club. I go upstairs and ask CJ if he'll come with me to answer some questions and help clear up what's going on. Cj comes with me without any problems and answers the questions and it turns out it was nothing to do with him. A couple of the guys from his table have walked down to see what's going on and they stand quietly by and chat to me about boxing stuff as they recognised me from the last Total Collision show.

Wouldn't you know it another call to the VIP area apparently involving Shane and his group? I get asked to go up as I know them and am the best candidate to talk to them. So off I go and it becomes apparent that some sort of incident has taken place. There is group of gypsies and assorted guests gathered around a couple of the security guards. The guys make a gap in the circle and let me through to talk to Shane. It turns out that Shane has tried to get past and couldn't lift his sleeve high enough to show his wristband and one of our foreign door staff has grabbed him. Shane hasn't fought back, but is merely standing his ground. It all gets sorted out and everyone goes back to what they were doing.

The problem is that Shane is pure traveller and for that reason alone people get anxious when he and his friends come into a club. They are generally no bother and I had never had a problem with him or any of the guys he brought in.

I go downstairs and get told by Church that he wants them all to leave. They are worried trouble might ensue. I say there isn't an issue and I am happy to run interference if anything else comes up. This isn't an option apparently.

The decision is out of my hands, but wouldn't you know it, it's my job to tell them all to leave. I go upstairs and ask to talk to Shane. I'm sat at the booth with him, all the travellers are stood around and the security is mixed in with them. Unsurprisingly Shane is not happy and we have a chat. He makes it very clear that they don't want to leave and they are not prepared to walk out and if we try to make them they'll be an issue and things will get physical. I explain that it's nothing personal, it's my job and I have to do what I'm told. We have an understanding that we both are prepared to fight if needs be, but it isn't anything personal and nothing will carry it on past the club.

COCAINE COMBAT

ADDICTED TO THE LIFE

Luckily for us when I go back downstairs to relay the message, Shane has decided to would be better if they all just left to avoid any incident. He walks out and shakes my hand. Sarah is stood on the front door and clicks 80 of them out. We were well and truly outnumbered and were lucky that they decided to leave as we were never going to get them out.

Here's where a club will show its true colours. Now some people who came in with Shane's group were not allowed in. We have an ID scanner at the club and it has to scan everyone that comes in. So some of the people who weren't allowed in got to skip the scanner and go through. After this incident with police being called and everything that was eventually averted. The police ask why these people were allowed in. We say we were overruled and the managers made the decision. We then got in trouble for not taking responsibility for letting the people in. One particular female manager said well you could have got us in trouble. Well the managers and owners are happy to overrule the door staff and let people in, but will not take responsibility when something goes wrong. It's us who have to take that, get fined up £1000 and possibly loose our licenses....fucking bollocks.

ADDICTED TO THE LIFE

One Last Run

    Church is off in Ibiza and I'm left to run the show at Halo for the week. I get my friend Ravi in for the week on loan from Cameo to help run the door with me.

    The night is the same as ever. A guy gets brought out early. He was problem last week and this week he has been kicking off in the club over something to do with his girlfriend apparently. So he does the smart thing and just stands outside running his mouth off and insulting everyone within in ear shot.

    We just ignore him as he's just a fucking gimp and is not posing any real danger to anyone. But he carries on for over an hour and a half with his never ending siege of abuse.

    At this point Ilker arrives with Khalid and they are stood outside chatting away about general stuff. Ilker calls over to Lauren our VIP manager and says his niece and her two friends are coming down to the club and can Lauren give some VIP wristbands when they arrive. The guy decides to shout his mouth off about this saying "yeah cos you want to fuck them." Ilker turns towards the guy and says what's your problem? The guy starts walking up to Ilker and saying what you gonna do about it? I step around from behind the barricade and grab the guy before he can put a hand on Ilker and take him to the floor, I slap him on the forehead a couple of times and say is this really what you want?

    Ravi and I had already called town watch to keep the cameras on him and they send us a message saying they have seen what's happened and have sent a unit to us to remove him.

    Over a week goes by and nothing is said about the incident involving the guy I took down. Suddenly I get a call from Church saying I need to come into the club. I arrive and apparently Amy wants to go over what happened as she has just found out about it. We go up to the CCTV room and go over the footage. I explain exactly what happens as it happens on the screen. She tries to argue that I should have waited instead of grabbing the guy before he could have struck Ilker. So I say you want me to wait for a guy to attack a member of staff first, rather than nullify the situation before one of the staff can get hurt?

    I don't think Amy appreciated my comments or making her sound stupid.

    The next day I am sat in the cafe next door to the club when my phone goes off and it is Church. He tells me that I have been fired from Halo due to the incident with the guy from the week before. I say is this a fucking joke and he says no. Apparently Amy sent the CCTV with a very unflattering email to the head of the security company we work for and they immediately fire me and ban me from over 260 of their venues and further more they call Church up and threaten to fire him and accuse him of deliberately hiding a 'violent incident' from the company. How fucking snake like can you be. Unfortunately Ty walked into the cafe at that precise moment and was not actually aware that I had been fired as Amy had acted on it on her own without informing anyone at the club.

COCAINE COMBAT

ADDICTED TO THE LIFE

So I'm sat in the hospital waiting room. I am in for blood tests to make sure I haven't anything got from biting part of that guy's finger off the night Bournemouth got promoted – you remember that bit - After a little wait I get called in and take my seat with my designated medical person. We get chatting and she asks me why I'm there. So I explain I'm a doorman and tell her about biting a part of the guys' finger off at the club. She looks at me with a startled expression and says "God you must have some stories to tell."

ADDICTED TO THE LIFE

Life After Doors – The Notorious S.E.B

When you've spent the majority of a decade doing something and then it suddenly stops you can end up becoming a bit lost. Now I'm not saying that my life doesn't work or isn't worth living without the chance to throw on a too tight high vis shirt and tell drunks to go fuck themselves, but it did leave me with a solid amount of free time to fill. And more importantly I had an income to replace.

Now I know I've hinted at times during this book about getting money by a few different ways and some of them may not have been the most legal at times. So I'm just gonna level with you here and tell you that without door work I went back to the one sure fire thing I knew how to do.

I was a month or so away from going back up to university and figured whilst I had some free time at weekends I would spend some time on the other side of the bar. This inevitably meant a return to my truest and oldest love the old Columbian bam bam, yayo, go-ee, snow, sniff, flake, marching powder, the old booga sugar.... COCAINE. The good thing about drugs is they are easily transported and freely (not free) available worldwide.

Back in the big smoke and at university beginning my final year. Things get quite serious when you hit your final year. When you have your final dissertation date it doesn't seem that big of a deal. You go back to uni in October and they tell you you best get cracking as the dissertation is only in May. May? Fuck off that's ages away. Fuck me it creeps up on you fast. And this year I was once again under the influence. Being that I was not working at weekends it gave me the option to zip back on forth between Bournemouth and London and this opened up a pretty sweet system. Bournemouth had a fucking infestation of coke dealers, but very little that could get Mandy. London had a lot of Mandy and weed dealers, but little to no coke dealers. So one went one way and one went the other (insert winky face.)

The middle aged drinking partner! Luckily for me going home was fairly easy. I had my car and just packed up at lunch time on Friday and did the journey home leaving me with plenty of time to get myself nice and fresh for a night out. Now those of you who've been paying attention will recognise the name Rossco. Ross and I got a long well and being a similar age naturally had a similar outlook on things. When you hit the 30 mark or approach it. You start to think a bit differently when you go out. Unlike most of the 20 year olds that are out, we have fuck all to prove. I'm not gonna snap and start fighting some kid just because he spilt something on my shoes or didn't say excuse me as he went past. I don't take that shit personally and neither did Ross. Plus we both very much liked women and the old sugar booga. So naturally we started to drink and party together.

Weeks were pretty set up without door work. If Ross was about then I would swing back to Bournemouth on the Friday and head back up Sunday afternoon. If things were busy with uni then I would just stay up in London and head out with the rugby league team on Friday night. Plus I had now downloaded tinder so, well, you know.

COCAINE COMBAT

ADDICTED TO THE LIFE

I fucking loved tinder. Every chic that had their about me as 'If you just want pussy pics or to fuck then don't message' yeah all of them just fucked. So easy to tell who was just pretending they weren't looking for a casual fuck. If you want a relationship you won't find it by just looking at someone's face on a mobile app.

In the run up to Christmas I did get talking to one of the hostesses from a club in Bournemouth. She was to be fair very attractive and despite what most people think of girls in the clubbing world she was classy. We ended up talking about my book that I was writing and things just went from there. We had a handful of dates. Our personalities could easily be described as slightly, almost completely polar opposites.

I was doing a lot of drinking and a lot coke over the festive period. The ironic thing being I was also training for a power lifting competition at the beginning of March. I would be on it all weekend and then roll up for my bench session on Monday at the Dungeon. Lee aka coach remarked more than once that I seemed to be better in the gym after a weekend bender than when I had spent the weekend just chilling out. It's funny how the body works.

Christmas came and went without much of a hoorah. I was partying hard and did enjoy one eventful night in town with a tattooed guy from the northern coast line from some 'reality' TV show. He wanted coke, I was in the club and had coke. 11 hours later our combined drinking and partying came to end. I'm still in his phone as Seb Yayo Bouncer. Ironically I was working in that particular club as bad Santa. Well I certainly made people happy with my sack of presents.

So with me being off the doors this meant that New Years was mine to do as I pleased this year. Luckily for me Rossco and a few of the boys decided to throw a fancy black and white attire house party away from the moronic hordes of pissed up nightclub goers. I got an extra tight fitting white jumper and a few bags of the only party accessory you'll need for New Years and off to the ball I went.

Spending a night not having to worry about drunks and retards trying to fight you or dealing with some chic who has puked on herself whilst simultaneously losing her knickers was a lovely change. I spent most of the night sniffing my brains out and actually interacting with people.

Essentially this is how New Years Eve really broke down. I arrived at pretty much bang on 7 when the party was said to start. I know the cool kids don't normally get there until late, but fuck it. I've got a night off; a couple cases of beer and enough snow to take me throw to next Christmas

The night was creeping along at a solid pace and people were turning up and adding to the general merriment of the situation. A couple hours in and my friend Stacey swings in. We'd bumped into each other earlier in the day and she said she would pop in whilst on route to a different New Years Eve party nearby. Long story short we spent the night chatting, drinking and keeping each other company and at around 3am when all the morons were returning from town beered up and ready to fight, we decided to leave.

ADDICTED TO THE LIFE

We end up at hers as it's nearby and carry on partying until around 6am and I then feel it's probably a good time to head home and actually get some sleep or at least attempt it as I'm wired off my nut. As I say good bye and give her a hug my mind suddenly races to one critical point. I had naired – that's a hair removal cream – balls and crack and if ever there was a time to go for a kiss, then fuck it this was it.

We spent the next couple of months going for food on proper dates and having what can be described as some rather aggressive sex. Considering I'm a shade under 6ft 2 and about 200lbs and Stacey was a shade over 5ft and about 100lbs I'm quite impressed she survived. If I've learnt anything from my misadventure of a life it is that you have to enjoy the moment. A couple months of enjoyment and fun with someone is worth more than 2 or 3 years of trying to force something with the wrong person.

Power lifting in Manchester. As mentioned earlier I had been prepping for a bench press competition. The competition was being held up in Manchester and dubbed 'Tattooed and Strong.' I had never entered a comp before and did my best to come in prepared. I had dieted and then gotten some bug, so I then had to try and bulk as I had dropped too much weight, the train up I didn't eat as I didn't know exactly what my weight was.

I arrived in Eccles to meet George and Abi, they were both competing. George was Coach Lee's son and a multi world record holder and Abi was George's girlfriend whom I also believe is a world record holder. I was an 88kg party animal who barely stayed sober long enough to take anything seriously, but this was different.

I had said to the bromance Scott that I would come up and compete in honour of Big Dave and although I hadn't competed before I could still bench 145kg in the gym and that would be enough to put on a decent showing.

The competition itself is spread over two days with the heavier weight classes going on the second day. I was on day one and to say the competition didn't really go my way would be an understatement. I bombed all three of my attempts and all for slightly different reasons. Failing wasn't necessarily the problem for me. Fuck it I had lost a cage fight, rugby matches, football matches, poker games and loads of shit before. I never claimed to be the perfect athlete nor did I think I was going to turn up and be some sort of undiscovered power lifting God. It was the fact this was an event I had attributed and dedicated to Dave and his memory. Failing so badly meant in my mind I had let him down and it was absolutely soul destroying. I walked off the platform after my final failed attempt and just hid in the men's room for a while, slowly trying to bring myself back into the room.

Back in the big smoke and focusing on the final dissertation for my degree. This was the bad boy that would make or break most people's hopes and dreams at a degree that could give them a worth while job – although my degree was in theatre so does it really count?

As all the various final groups were tweaking and revising their final performance, the last impression they would leave behind after 3 years of hard work and crippling financial debt – thanks conservative party you two faced cunts. One thing seemed abundantly clear. The

ADDICTED TO THE LIFE

females on my course seemed to be obsessed with nudity. Nearly every group of females seemed to think that they had to make some big grandioso gesture and make a stand for women everywhere by getting their tits and hoo-ha out on stage. Now I had made a name for myself for being essentially half naked in at least one performance a year if not a term. So how would one top that... Fuck it we were going to have to go balls out, literally. The story we were telling would suit having a nude scene in it and wouldn't make it seem like we were just throwing one in for the shock factor.

So to mark the end of my university journey that week in May will be one for the memory books. The year anniversary of Big Dave's funeral, my dissertation the day after and Mums birthday the day after that. One of the more interesting weeks of my life for varying reasons. Oh and just in case you're keeping score I left university with BA Theatre 2.1.

What's that? I can finally have my license back... What's that? The club where I was fired from, resulting in my nationwide ban have got rid of the snakey wench that fucked me over want me back? Could it be...

Printed in Great Britain
by Amazon